T0400534

Resisting English Hegemony

Anti-colonial Educational Perspectives for Transformative Change

The titles published in this series are listed at *brill.com/acep*

Resisting English Hegemony

A Study of Five English as a Foreign Language (EFL)
High School Teachers

By

Ewa Barbara Krawczyk

BRILL

SENSE

LEIDEN | BOSTON

All chapters in this book have undergone peer review.

The Library of Congress Cataloging-in-Publication Data is available online at http://catalog.loc.gov

Typeface for the Latin, Greek, and Cyrillic scripts: "Brill". See and download: brill.com/brill-typeface.

ISSN 2542-9280
ISBN 978-90-04-39436-0 (paperback)
ISBN 978-90-04-38973-1 (hardback)
ISBN 978-90-04-39437-7 (e-book)

I humbly dedicate this work to my beloved mother Małgorzata Renata Krawczyk, who was the first educator in my life from the day I was born, and who would sacrifice anything for my wellbeing.

∴

Contents

Preface

Self as Researcher

During the years of my education, which took place during communism (1945–1989) in Poland (Glassheim, 2006), classrooms were simple, hardly exposing any students' work. Textbooks were greyish and boring. Students were forced to learn the Russian language from the age of ten. Classes were authoritarian, teacher-centered, and the teachers used rulers to hit students on their hands if they misconducted. The early 1980s were critical and challenging for people who had children in school. The Polish people not only had to use ration stamps for food, but even for school supplies: notebooks, erasers, pencils and such.

With the fall of communism, which took place in Poland in 1989 (Odrowaz, 2009), the borders opened and teachers and their students experienced Western exposure. Times changed. Textbooks became more colorful and inviting. The teaching methods became more student-centered. After I graduated from college with a degree to teach English as a Foreign Language (EFL), I became a teacher of the English language in a public school in my hometown in 1993.

In 1999, I immigrated to the United States. This significant change gave me a whole new perspective into my personal life, as well as my educational and professional goals and aspirations. While living in Poland, I belonged to the demographic majority having a high status in Polish society by virtue of the position of my family and my education. However, the moment I put my foot on the American soil, I felt I was instantly 'boxified' and classified into the category of "the other." It was not only a very eye-opening experience to me, but by shifting from a homogenous, mono-linguistic and mono-religious culture into a very diverse, multi-dimensional, heterogeneous, complex and dynamic hybridized culture; I underwent a process of personal transformation and awakening. Not until I became a resident of this country did I realize the challenges and complexities of the culturally and linguistically diverse society that the American society presents.

Through this process and my work with people pushed to the margins of society: people with learning disabilities, homeless individuals and refugees in the United States, I gained new perspectives, new experiences, new opportunities and new challenges – factors that have decidedly made me a better person – more tolerant, open, empathetic, understanding, compassionate, and a more knowledgeable educator. I can describe this as a shift in my entire being.

Through my work with the marginalized I have come to realize even more profoundly the importance of educating myself, as well as others, and the need for reforms in the educational system. Thus, I came to the conclusion to pursue my education in the United States in order to deepen and satisfy my strong interests in critical pedagogies, multicultural education, curriculum for a diverse society, and the education of immigrants in this country.

In 2007, I graduated with a B.A. from the University of Massachusetts in Boston (UMass Boston) majoring in American Studies. The American Studies courses that focused on American history, culture, and society were very enlightening to me and awoke my curiosity about the education of minorities, social justice, poverty, economics, inequality, suppression, asymmetrical power relations, and pseudo-globalization. As a result, I decided to pursue my education even further by entering the graduate program in Applied Linguistics majoring in Teaching English as a Second Language (TESL) also at UMass Boston. I obtained my M.A. in May of 2009. In the course of majoring in TESL at the graduate level, I was exposed to various issues relating to language, such as language development, language acquisition, bilingualism, biculturalism, as well as issues concerning the contemporary use of English.

The works of Paolo Freire, Donaldo Macedo, bell hooks, James Gee, Henry Giroux, John Ogbu, Lilia Bartolomé, Gloria Anzaldúa, Pepi Leistyna and others, have significantly contributed to my intellectual development. The social factors expressed by these authors do not seem to be a part of a typical curriculum in language teacher preparation and, as a result, many elementary, middle and high school, and even college teachers fail to realize and appreciate the influence of these socio-cultural and sociolinguistic factors in their professional teaching of language. I desire to contribute my post-doctoral energies towards changing and correcting this situation.

All the experiences described above, my research assignments, and the support and inspiration from my professors in the Department of Applied Linguistics at UMass Boston shaped my desire to pursue my doctoral studies. I applied to the Ph.D. program in Curriculum and Instruction, because I realized the potential of scholarly work and the influence that this field of study can have on the teaching practices in the American educational system and institutions. Such scholarly work is also necessary to enlighten policy makers who have the power to control what educational programs to support or not to support, as their decisions may consequently determine the future of millions of students. This is especially true for those who are pushed to the margins of society: the poor, the disabled, the intellectually challenged, the voluntary and involuntary immigrants, and culturally and linguistically diverse learners.

My education, my linguistic and cultural background, and my teaching EFL and English as a Second (ESL) experience have made me very sensitive to these issues. I am passionate and serious about making a difference by changing society through critical thinking and pedagogies. My doctoral degree provides me with the necessary research skills, gives me credibility in the face of decision makers, enables me to be a more effective teacher/researcher, and allows me to sustain and broaden my intellectual horizons.

I have great enthusiasm for the opportunity to have worked closely with professors such as Dr. Karin Wiburg, Dr. Myriam Torres, Dr. Jeanette Haynes Writer, Dr. Oakley Hadfield, Dr. Rudolfo Chávez Chávez, Dr. Hermán García and Dr. David Rutledge at New Mexico State University (NMSU), who equipped me with the necessary skills to become an effective researcher and practitioner in the field of language teaching, particularly in multicultural and multilingual contexts. I have learned first-hand the importance of studying with individuals who challenge and enthuse their students. It is their intellectual energy in literacy and language education that has given me inspiration to imagine a different teacher, a teacher and a scholar in one person who understands the importance of teaching with an individualistic approach, understanding, having empathy and compassion towards learners.

During my education at UMass Boston and NMSU I also learned that education is not a "neutral enterprise" (Apple, 2004, p. 1), schools are not neutral institutions, and that they perpetuate a certain ideology promoting some cultures and devaluing others, either consciously or unconsciously. Therefore, I learned the importance of sensitivity, empathy and awareness of the issues that culturally and linguistically diverse students bring to the classroom every day. I also have a strong desire to pass this sensitivity, empathy, compassion and awareness onto other students and future educators.

My desire was to conduct research for my dissertation in Poland (see Figure 1), as I had not lived there for 17 years. I was curious how the political changes in the country such as the fall of communism and the European Union membership influenced education, especially when it comes to EFL education. Living and being educated in the United States I have learned about modern and progressive teaching methodologies and the importance of developing speaking, communicative, and cooperative skills in students by their teachers. These are skills that help students in their future professional careers to communicate effectively, successfully work in teams and feel comfortable, and be confident in public speaking situations. Thus, I was interested if and to what extent teachers in Poland made a shift into modern and progressive methodologies geared towards developing students' speaking, communicative, and cooperative skills.

Summary

Not until I became an immigrant in the United States and a graduate student in this country did I gain a theoretical and a practical knowledge of many factors, which contribute to the successful development of speaking, communicative, and cooperative skills in a language other than the native language. Therefore, in my research I desired to investigate and uncover the various factors leading to the development of the English language in Polish students and EFL students in the EFL context. I focused on the factors that could be changed, such as methodology and attitudes used in the EFL classroom. I strongly believe my findings can benefit EFL students, teachers, administrators, curriculum creators, and policy makers.

Map of Poland

Acknowledgements

I would like to thank my brother Michał Krawczyk and his wife Gracjana Krawczyk, my sister Kornelia Nierobisch and her husband Ryszard Nierobisch for their motivation and support. Unfortunately, death took Ryszard before he was able to see this work published.

I would like to thank my niece Tatiana Krawczyk, my nephews: Tymoteusz Krawczyk and Carsten Nierobisch, and my Goddaughter Dominika Frączek for their smiles and thinking about me during the writing process.

I would like to thank my dear friends: Aleksandra Kwiecień, Jadwiga Milewska-Connolly, Aneta Kalicka, Joanna Dyzio, Br. Julian Miller, Brian Dunn, Marius Zakarauskas, and my dear graduate studies' friends: Dr. Michelle Saenz-Adames, Dr. Ashley Ryan, Dr. Su-Jin Choi, Dr. Loretta Wideman, Dr. Lihua Zhang, and Jennifer Green for their listening ears and words of encouragement.

I would like to thank my doctoral studies professors: Dr. Karin Wiburg, Dr. David Rutledge, Dr. Patricia MacGregor-Mendoza, Dr. Lilian Rogers de Cibils, and Dr. Oakley Hadfield for their patience, guidance and encouraging me to move forward.

I would like to thank Dr. Donaldo Macedo from the University of Massachusetts in Boston for believing in me and "fishing me out of the crowd" to believe and encourage me to do doctoral studies.

I would like to thank all of the University of Massachusetts faculty and staff in Boston for teaching me about progressive multicultural education and all of the New Mexico State University faculty and staff in Las Cruces for teaching me how to think and write critically about education.

I would also like to thank the five participants of this work, as without you ladies, this book would not be written.

Finally, I would like to thank my friend Amanda for her special support and Dr. Stacey Duncan, Brady Richards, and Gaspard Mucundanyi for editing this study.

I appreciate all of you for being there for me!

Note on the Author

Ewa Barbara Krawczyk received her PhD from the College of Education specializing in Curriculum and Instruction, Bilingual Education, Teaching English to Speakers of Other Languages (TESOL) and Educational Learning Technologies at New Mexico State University in Las Cruces, New Mexico. Ewa was born and raised in communist and post-communist Poland where she graduated from Teachers' College of English and was a teacher of English as a foreign language in a public high school in the years 1993–1999. She immigrated to the United States in 1999 where she gained her personal experience through her work with adult individuals with intellectual disabilities in Seattle, Washington and Boston, Massachusetts areas, and homeless, immigrant, and refugee women with children in Seattle. Ewa obtained her educational experience through receiving Bachelor's degree in American Studies in 2007 and Master's degree in Applied Linguistics, majoring in Teaching English as a Second Language in 2009, both at the University of Massachusetts in Boston. In spring 2015 Ewa conducted a research for three months in Poland observing and interviewing five English as a foreign language public high school teachers focusing on the ways the teachers manifest their pedagogies in developing their students' communicative, and cooperative skills with a particular focus on language production, which resulted in publication of this book. Ewa's interests include multiculturalism, diversity, bilingual education, TESOL (Teaching English to Speakers of Other Languages), social justice issues, immigration issues and policies, culture, society, sociolinguistics, psycholinguistics, second language acquisition and the use of technology in the process of teaching and learning. During the years: 2016–2018 Ewa taught developmental English at the College of the Marshall Islands in Majuro, the capital of the Republic of Marshall Islands, South Pacific. Presently, Ewa lives in Seattle, where she teaches English to immigrants and refugees. Checks Ewa's other recent publications:

DeCoursey, C. A., & Krawczyk, E. B. (2017). The major in cultural context: Choosing liberal arts in the Marshall Islands. *English Language Teaching: Canadian Center of Science and Education, 10*(11), 214–228. Retrievable from http://www.ccsenet.org/journal/index.php/elt/article/view/71338

Krawczyk, E. B. (2016). Comparative discourse analysis: Dichotomous reality from a polish immigrant's perspective. In P. W. Orelus (Ed.), *Language, race, and power in schools: A critical discourse analysis* (Ch. 12, pp. 171–181). New York, NY: Routledge. Routledge Research in Education Series. Retrieved from https://www.amazon.com/Language-Race-Power-Schools-Discourse-ebook/dp/B01N1Q6B02/ref=sr_1_2?ie=UTF8&qid=1542498859&sr=8-2&keywords=pierre+orelus

CHAPTER 1

Introduction

Historical Overview

Throughout history foreign language learning has always been an important practical concern (Richards & Rogers, 2014). Five hundred years ago Latin was the language to teach and learn, as it was the dominant language of education, commerce, religion, and government in the Western world. Kielar (1972) points out that in the 17th century besides Latin, French was the primary language in Europe, including Poland. However, it changed. Through the last decades teaching and learning English became more popular in Europe and an increasing amount of research has surfaced concerning the teaching, learning and the use of English in different European contexts (e.g., Berns, 1995; Cenoz & Jessner, 2000; Phillipson & Skutnab-Kangas, 1997; Van Essen, 1997), and incorporating literature regarding English in Central and Eastern Europe (e.g. Dushku, 1998; Fonzari, 1999; McCallen, 1991; O'Reilly, 1998; Petzold & Berns, 2000; Schleppegrell, 1991).

As mentioned by English for Specific Purposes (1975), English has been the language of business, technology, marketing, commerce, science, aviation, mining, engineering, agriculture, and marine research. English is also the most desired language to learn and teach in countries outside of the English as a first language speaking discourse (Crystal, 2012). The English language is the world's most widely studied foreign language as well because English is the most popular language of communication in the world among native and non-native speakers of English (Richards & Rogers, 2014). As far as Poland is concerned, "Poland is a linguistically uniform country in which Polish is the official language used to communicate in all spheres of public and social life" (Czura & Papaja, 2013, p. 322). As far as the English language's presence in Poland is concerned, Reichelt (2005) writes "English-language instruction was first introduced in the 18th century in Eastern Poland, and the first English handbook was published in 1780" (p. 217).

In the late 18th century Poland was partitioned among Russia, Prussia and Austria-Hungary. Russian and German were state and school official languages until the end of World War I in 1918. During this time Polish was moved to the status of the second category, a language spoken only in Polish homes, but forbidden in schools and other official institutions. After the World War II, the Polish language regained its high status in Poland. The status of English started

© KONINKLIJKE BRILL NV, LEIDEN, 2019 | DOI:10.1163/9789004394377_001

to change as well. Fisiak (1985) says that during the interwar period between World War I and World War II there were only 120 students majoring in English at Polish universities and in 1955 the number grew to only 150 students. After Joseph Stalin's death in 1953 (Wines, 2003), Poland experienced a slight thaw of communism in the country. In 1959/1960 academic year there were about 350 students majoring in English in Poland (Fisiak, 1994). From the 1960s and on, university English programs in Poland received help in the form of lecturers, textbooks, periodicals and scholarships from the British and the American Embassies in the capital of Poland, Warsaw.

The Russian language superseded the native Polish language in elementary and high schools in the country. After World War II the Russian language was required to be studied by all students. Janowski (1992) commenting on the role of the Russian language in Poland indicates "...the Russian language was adopted as the primary foreign language to be instructed to all students from the age of 11 and upwards, regardless of the kind of institution" (p. 43). Later, English was introduced as a compulsory subject in public schools in the early 1960s (Reichelt, 2005). The instruction of English was described as "... dull, overloaded programs detached from reality, unfunctional syllabuses and drab, boring books..." (Ehrenhalt, 1990, p. 8).

The role of English in Poland in the 1960s and the 1970s was somewhat limited in that, it "...was offered as a second foreign language only to pupils attending full secondary school, in other words, institutions leading to a school leaving certificate" (Janowski, 1992, p. 43). Various cultural and educational institutions offered evening English classes outside of the public school system during the time of communism, however, the classes were oversized and the instructional materials were poor, as a result most student were uninterested in studying the English language (Ehrenhalt, 1990).

Studying English became more popular in Poland in the 1970s, as young Poles saw learning English as means of expressing solidarity with the West and resistance to the Soviet influence (Muchisky, 1985). In the 1980s the popularity of English continued to grow. According to the British Council (1986), in the 1980s English was the most important foreign language studied in Poland. It was more important than studying e.g. German, French, Spanish or Italian. From the 1989–1990 academic year onward the learning of Russian ceased to be compulsory, and, at about the same time, the Polish government began to encourage the widespread teaching of West European languages in schools (Janowski, 1992).

In the 1980s, interest in learning English continued to increase and there was a demand in Poland for foreign languages, English in particular. For example, three or four days in advance of registration for English courses at the Methodist Centre, which had the reputation for offering the best English-language instruction, the lines formed in Warsaw's Constitution Square (Varney, 1984). During the 1980s and the 1990s, students of English in Poland started believing that their knowledge of English could help them in their future careers and economic status. Varney (1984) says:

> Teaching of English in Poland is very good. It is, of course much easier to teach when you know that your pupils and students *want* to learn. Motivation of students and teachers is high. Materials are few and far between; even Polish texts (and the Poles really prefer authentic materials from Britain) are limited by a shortage of paper for printing. Teachers and students are alike, though adept at adaptation, are really hungry for EFL materials from the West.... However, even the considerable British Council resources cannot totally meet the unbelievable demand for English, English...and more English. (p. 155)

English teachers had higher numbers of students in their classes including a large number of students who desired to learn English very quickly. Also, Polish students' traditionally had to learn English in a way that involved seemingly unappealing methods. Muchisky (1985) points out:

> Poland represents a situation in which virtually all English proficiency is developed in formal classroom settings. And those classrooms violate literally every principle considered central to good classroom learning: the classrooms are overcrowded, attention is focused upon grammar and pronunciation drills, the relationship between teachers and students can best be described as adversarial, there is continual error correction and a heavy emphasis on rote learning with little concern for meaningful involvement on the part of the learner. In addition, because of the current political and economic situation in Poland, access to native speakers of English and classroom materials in English is limited. Yet in spite of these limitations, Polish students develop a high level of English proficiency. (p. 2)

The fall of communism opened up access to new materials and pedagogies for Polish teachers. Seeing the Western countries having shifted teaching of English towards the Communicative Approach put teachers of English in Poland in a situation where they had to explore a new teaching methodology, establish new courses, and find or create teaching material suitable to the new educational, social, political, cultural, and economic situation in Poland. This was an educational, political, economic and cultural shift of a paradigm. As pointed out by Kuhn (1996) "The decision to reject one paradigm is always simultaneously the decision to accept another..." (p. 79).

Definitions of Terms

There are four notions to be explained for a better understanding of this research: English as a Foreign Language versus English as a Second Language, realia, and mind map.

English as a Foreign Language versus English as a Second Language

The terms English as a Foreign Language (EFL) and English as a Second Language (ESL), are often mistakenly used as interchangeable notions by numerous educators, teachers, authors, researchers, and scholars. There are two main differences between EFL and ESL: the location where English is being taught to speakers of other languages, and the students who are being taught (Kallenberger, 2011). For example, an American living and teaching English in Poland is an EFL teacher. His or her students are most likely to be of Polish origin and their first language is most likely to be Polish as well. These students study EFL in a formal school setting for a certain number of hours per week from elementary to high school and college/university levels. These students are the majority in their own country, and they have full citizen rights. The Polish language has a high status and is commonly used on a daily basis in Poland in all aspects of daily life. It is "...the essential ingredient of Polish nationality" (Volenski & Grzymala-Moszczynska, 1997, p. 330) and Polish is the language of government, commerce, science, and culture (Zimmerman, 2010).

As opposed to EFL, a teacher living and teaching English in an Anglo country, such as the U.S., Canada, Australia, New Zealand, Great Britain, or Ireland is teaching ESL. The teacher's students are most likely to be students, who are from non-English-speaking countries and now living and studying English in a native English-speaking country. The English language learners (ELL) may be living permanently as immigrants in the country or may just be visiting the country for a limited amount of time.

Many ESL learners are immigrants in native English-speaking countries and have no desire to return to their native countries. Their status is different from EFL learners. Many of them struggle financially. They might feel inferior, as they represent a minority in their new country. Their native language might be looked down upon. They might experience a culture shock, as their culture might vary from the Anglo culture. ESL students who come from poor countries are often stigmatized as language learners that cost a lot of money to the government of a given native English speaking country. ESL learners often are perceived as poor, dirty, lazy, violent, not intelligent, and uneducated (Yosso, 2002). In both cultural and social EFL and ESL contexts, the expectation to learn English is very different, and this has deep implications for teaching. While EFL students learn English for their own advancement and to develop professionally, for ESL students learning English is usually a matter of survival and becoming a part of the new culture.

Realia

"…the word realia means using real items found in the world around us to help teach English. Using realia, helps to make English lessons memorable, creating a link between the objects, and the word or phrase they show" (TEFL Survival, n.d.). According to dictionary.com (n.d.), realia are "objects, as coins, tools, etc., used by a teacher to illustrate everyday living."

Mind Map

Buzan (1983) defines mind map as an information organizer, which arranges information into a form that is easily assimilated by the brain and consequently more easily remembered and recalled. According to Herrera et al. (2011), mind map is generally used to produce, visualize, structure, and classify thoughts and ideas using words and images, and it supports comprehension and cognition as it brings a hands-on device to learners, which can be utilized during lessons. A mind map is a tool that also helps learners to monitor their own understanding, focus on key concepts, and make connections from known knowledge to unknown knowledge. It fosters social growth and motivates learners to learn from others around them (Herrera et al., 2011).

Background of the Study

My experience as an EFL high school teacher in my native country of Poland, my experience as an immigrant in the United States, and my educational experience as a student in this country at all college levels (bachelor's, master's and doctoral), have made me reflect on my past experiences as a learner and a teacher of EFL. My experience as a learner of EFL in Poland took place about 35 years ago in a school setting during the communist government era. My experience as an EFL teacher took place about 20 years ago, a few years after the fall of communism in Poland. During these times, Polish teachers and learners of English had limited access to teaching methodologies, teaching materials, and technology already widely used in native English-speaking countries. During these times, there was a common understanding by the Polish educational authorities of the importance of focusing on the reading and writing skills in the English language, as grammatical correctness was in center of teaching English. Therefore, the commonly used approach in teaching the English language was the Grammatical/Grammar-Based Approach. This model was perpetuated through generations of teachers and students because the Polish educational authorities strongly emphasized checking students' knowledge and progress through standardized testing, such as: written grammar and vocabulary memorization-oriented tests and quizzes. The Grammatical/Grammar-Based Approach suited the purpose of teaching English without regarding the development of students' speaking, communicative, and cooperative skills in the communist era. Speaking on the emphasis on testing in education, Schlechty (2011), says "Beating the goal becomes beating the test rather than educating children" (p. 43).

As a result of this situation, teachers and students in the 1980s heavily depended on textbooks loaded with reading and writing materials and were scarcely using materials and methods that would contribute to the development of EFL learners' speaking, communicative, and cooperative skills. Polish teachers of English worked with what they had available: unappealing and uninteresting English textbooks designed by non-native speakers of English, and censored according to the communist indoctrination. The textbooks were modeled according to the Grammatical/Grammar-Based Approach and its methods common in ancient times, when students were required to learn Latin and Greek. EFL teachers in Poland had almost no access to audio and visual materials.

Therefore, the EFL students in Poland were able to achieve quite a satisfactory level of English when it comes to grammar, reading, and writing skills, as observed by researchers and statisticians. However, by being minimally exposed to speaking, communicative, and cooperative practices and by not being surrounded by the English language on a daily basis, they lacked the knowledge of English in the areas of speaking, communication, and cooperation.

The Need to Understand Changes in EFL Teaching

Students develop their speaking, communicative, and cooperative skills in English through interaction and participation in pair and group activities in the classroom. These interactive activities lead not only to the increase of students' speaking, communicative, and cooperative skills for the purpose of learning the English language, but these are also skills students can utilize after high school graduation as employers and employees. The students will be able to talk more confidently in the professional world, e.g. at meetings and conferences, they will be able to be more skilled leaders in a professional environment, and they will become equipped with better skills to work in teams with more flexibility and negotiating skills. As Bowman and Plaisir (1996) say "Teamwork is essential to the success of the projects and student realize that they must work together if they are to complete the activities" (p. 27).

The English language has been present in Polish secondary schools for several decades. In the times of communism, it was not as common as it is today, where every Polish high school student has to learn English. The intention of school authorities is to prepare EFL students to be fluent in the four literacy areas: listening, speaking, reading and writing. As mentioned before, because of the strong emphasis on reading, and writing grammatically and stylistically correct English, there was little attention paid to the development of students' speaking, communicative, and cooperative skills.

As an experienced teacher of EFL, a citizen of an Anglo country, and a doctoral student studying the role of Teaching English to Speakers of Other Languages (TESOL), I was very curious how in practice the political, societal, economic, and educational changes in Poland influenced the ways EFL teachers approach, engage, and teach their students in Poland now. One of the benefits of this dissertation is the opportunity to compare teaching English during the communist period and now, when communism is no longer part of Poland, with a particular focus on developing Polish EFL students' speaking, communicative, and cooperative skills by their teachers.

I felt there was a need to explore how the political, social, economic, cultural, and educational changes in Poland impacted English teachers and how the changes have been influencing methodologies in their teaching-learning dynamics. The study can be informative for EFL educators from other countries as well, especially that the teaching English methodology in Poland is rather unknown by Teaching English to Speakers of Other Languages educators in English and non-English speaking countries and the information from my study can enrich the research in both EFL and ESL areas.

The Purpose and the Significance of the Study

My purpose of this study was to observe and interview five participating teachers and learn what their paths were in becoming EFL teachers and to examine how they teach EFL today with a focus on developing their students' speaking, communicative, and cooperative skills. I was also interested in how the teaching of English changed from the communist era to the current period.

My intention was also to observe and examine how EFL high school instructors in Poland teach their students and share my research findings with other members in the EFL field so they will be able to take consideration and incorporate my research and enhance and enrich in this way their teaching-learning methodologies in their institutions and communities.

This research will also be informative and helpful to EFL instructors in additional countries where English is spoken, and teachers at English instruction schools, universities and colleges in such countries as the United States, Canada, Australia, New Zealand, Great Britain and Ireland. Thanks to the findings in my research, these instructors will be able to realize what Polish EFL teachers do or do not do in terms of enhancing their foreign learners' skills in the English language. Thus, through adjustments and a focus on needed areas of English language teaching and learning, instructors of English can help students be more successful in their educational journeys. I am positive such changes will lead to a greater awareness and fluency in EFL among the students in Poland and other countries.

My findings are not going to be used for the purpose of the dissertation only. The findings will be made public, thus EFL teachers, curriculum designers and policy makers in not only Poland, but also other non-native and native English-speaking countries can benefit from the findings and design their curricula. I am positive that by using my research they will be able to design their syllabi accordingly, and tailor their teaching methods so EFL students can learn in conditions in which there is optimal development of literacy skills in the English language with a particular focus on speaking, communication, and cooperation.

Research Question

This qualitative case study researched five English as a Foreign Language (EFL) public high school teachers in Poland, considered their stories of learning English, and examined the ways they manifest their pedagogical practices to develop and enhance their students' speaking, communicative, and cooperative skills in the English language. The overarching question for the research is: How do five EFL teachers in Poland manifest their pedagogical practices? This general research question contained several sub-questions.

Sub-question 1) What kinds of experience and educational preparation do the five Polish EFL teachers have?

Sub-question 2) How do Polish EFL teachers describe their EFL methodologies as related to their students' speaking, communicative, and cooperative skills, and how is their philosophy manifested in a classroom setting?

Sub-question 3a) How do these EFL teachers reflect on teaching practices prior to and subsequent to the fall of communism?

Sub-question 3b) Given that there are social, economic, and pedagogical differences in EFL pre- and post-communism, what evidence do the teachers provide that their practices in teaching EFL have changed over time?

Data to answer these questions was collected through semi-structured interviews and observations in the classrooms of five teachers. The information received from the five participating teachers was analyzed, compared, synthesized, and conclusions were drawn. A more detailed description of the interview protocols is presented in Chapter 3.

Summary

In Chapter 1, I outlined the historical overview of the teaching and learning foreign language situation in Poland with a particular focus on the English language. I also defined some terms present through the course of this study. Next, I described the background of the study, including my own experience as an EFL learner and a teacher, and the political, cultural, socio-economic and educational changes that influence teaching EFL in Poland. In this chapter, I also presented the purpose, significance and research question of this study.

Literature Review

Introduction

> Learning a second language is a long and complex undertaking. Your whole person is affected as you struggle to reach beyond the confines of your first language and into a new language, a new culture, a new way of thinking, feeling, and acting. Total commitment, total involvement, a total physical, intellectual, and emotional response are necessary to successfully send and receive messages in a second language. (Brown, 2006, p. 1)

As mentioned in my previous chapter, there has been motivating pressure on Polish society to learn English, especially since the fall of communism in 1989. Presently, English is taught in every public and private elementary, middle, and high school in Poland. Substantial amounts of money are poured into the English language educational system. Polish students who are fortunate enough to be able to spend some time in Anglo countries, being in the natural environment of the English language, make progress in mastering their speaking, communicative, and cooperative English language skills. Unfortunately, the majority of Polish students learning English who do not have the opportunities to practice their English listening and speaking abilities being confined to their classrooms only. The majority of Polish students, who graduate from high school or even university and have been learning English for several years, master grammar, however they are often not able to hold a substantial conversation in English.

When I lived in Poland in the 1990s, I was able to attend a college preparing me to be a professional EFL teacher. I had about 25 in-class hours of the English language and content knowledge conducted in English. During my classes students were not allowed to use Polish at all. My college employed native speakers of English from Great Britain and the United States for conversational and pronunciation classes. Throughout these years, I successfully developed proficiency in English grammar, phonetics, and all the four academic skills: listening, reading, writing, and speaking. Those skills helped me to assimilate into American society when I immigrated to the United States in 1999. I noticed that a majority Polish people who took regular EFL courses during their high school and college years in Poland as I had, were not able

© KONINKLIJKE BRILL NV, LEIDEN, 2019 | DOI:10.1163/9789004394377_002

to gain proficiency in English. Those whom I met in the United States were anxious to use English verbally and struggled with correct pronunciation. It is not a surprise, knowing the fact that speaking in a second or foreign language has often been viewed as the most demanding of the four skills (Bailey & Savage, 1994).

In order to gain a more profound understanding of the EFL and ESL teaching methods I experienced in Poland as a student and teacher, I felt I needed to understand the present theories and methods of foreign language/second language acquisition (FLA/SLA). Many courses at the University of Massachusetts in Boston, where I accomplished a Master's degree in Applied Linguistics and New Mexico State University, where I was specializing in Bilingual Education and Teaching English to Speakers of Other Languages included the very subject. The knowledge of concepts of second language acquisition approaches and methodologies by teachers will benefit the learning process of Polish students learning English, their teachers, their parents, and the broader community. I had no previous knowledge of Polish teachers' level of knowledge on contemporary EFL and ESL methodology and how they put it into practice in their classrooms. Through this study I connected the three approaches to teaching EFL and ESL, and the philosophical orientations as defined by Herrera and Murry (2011), who say "An approach is the philosophical orientation to instruction that serves as a guide for choosing among methods that are considered to be consistent with the tenets of the theory and scientifically based research that ground the theory" (p. 189). There are three main approaches in FLA/SLA: Grammatical/Grammar-Based, Communicative, and Cognitive (Herrera & Murry, 2011). In this literature review, in addition to the main FLA/SLA teaching and learning approaches, I present other teaching-learning themes such as: a process of democratization in Poland, the use of technology in instruction, student-centered instruction and teaching, and learning in an authentic environment.

Grammatical/Grammar-Based Approach

The Grammatical/Grammar-Based Approach is a teacher-centered approach. It has an assumption that students learn a foreign/second language best by memorization of its linguistic rules and sentence structures. Also, classes frequently overused the text and lecture format, which results in student memorization of facts and spitting them out on tests (Barba, 1997; Mayer, 1996). Herrera and Murry (2011) point out, "Learners study these rules and patterns in ways that are often isolated from a meaningful context" (p. 195).

The Grammatical/Grammar-Based Approach has been used since ancient times, when students were learning Latin and Greek and up until the middle of the 20th century (Brown, 2014). Today the Grammatical/Grammar-Based Approach is considered to be an old-fashioned historical artifact (Canale, 1983; Cummins, 2001; Krashen, 1981; Ovando & Collier, 2011; Wong Fillmore & Valdez, 1986).

Richards and Rogers (2007), commenting on the grammar translation component of the Grammatical/Grammar-Based Approach, say that the goal of foreign language study is to learn a language in order to read its literature, or in order to benefit from the mental discipline and intellectual development that result from foreign language study. Grammar translation is a way of studying a language that approaches the language first through detailed analysis of its grammar rules, followed by application of this knowledge to the task of translating sentences and texts into and out of the foreign/second, also referred to as a target language.

The native (first) language is maintained as the reference system in the acquisition of the second language. Reading and writing are the major focuses; little or no systematic attention is paid to speaking or listening. Vocabulary selection is based solely on the used reading materials, and words are taught through bilingual word lists, dictionary study, and memorization. Grammar is taught deductively. The students' native languages are the medium of instruction (Richards & Rogers, 2014).

Another trend within the Grammatical/Grammar-Based Approach was to focus less on explicit instruction of grammar and structure, and more on drills, repetitions, and memorization (Herrera & Murry, 2011). Students learned grammar and vocabulary through exposure to the target language only, which sometimes was time consuming, as simple translation would be more efficient. Translation and the use of native language was heavily discouraged. The first language of students was seen as an obstacle in acquiring and learning the foreign/second language. The instruction depended more on fluency of the language by teachers (native and native like teachers of the language) than on textbooks and teaching (Herrera & Murry, 2011).

Another component of the Grammatical/Grammar-Based Approach was a focus on drills and dialog designed to develop and enhance vocabulary, and grammatical structures. When language learners practiced the structures and dialogs, they would develop new structures, and it would become a habit. In other words, language acquisition was the memorization and recall of language patterns (Richards & Rogers, 2001). A teacher's role was to reinforce accurate language production in their students and error correction was done through consistent feedback (Terrell et al., 1982).

Link between the Study, the Grammatical/Grammar-Based
Approach and its Methodology

My study is related to the Grammatical/Grammar-Based Approach and its methodology, as it was the approach and methodology used in teaching-learning foreign language in Poland during the communist era, when the "Iron Curtain" acted like a "non-permeable membrane." As communism was approaching its end, the "Iron Curtain" became more like the process of osmosis enabling more modern and revolutionary teaching methodologies flow into the country from countries such as the United States, Great Britain, and Australia, which were leading in progressive foreign language teaching and learning methodologies.

In examining the development of Polish students' speaking, communicative, and cooperative skills in the English language by their teachers, I was interested if any aspects of the Grammatical/Grammar-Based Approach and its methodology are still used in English classrooms in Poland, and how they affect their development of English speaking, communicative, and cooperative abilities.

Communicative Approach

The Communicative Approach to teaching EFL and ESL emerged in the 1960s and, as the name suggests, communication lies at its core. Learners use language for purpose. Therefore, the role of the teacher and the students is to provide a context for authentic communication, as memorizing patterns does not do much for the process of learning a foreign/second language (Herrera & Murry, 2011). Instead, language development takes place when students obtain comprehensive input and when they interact in an authentic, low-anxiety, risk-free, and language-abundant environments (Blair, 1982; Terrell, 1991). The Communicative Approach to language teaching places emphasis on what learners know and can do with language, as well as what they want and need to do (Savignon, 1983).

Menezes (2008) highlights that, based on Vygotskian theories, language learning is a socially mediated process. Mediation is a fundamental principle, and language is a cultural artifact that mediates social and psychological activities. As Mitchell and Myles (2004) point out, "From a socio-cultural perspective, children's early language learning arises from processes of meaning-making in collaborative activity with other members of a given culture" (p. 200). Lantolf and Thorne (2007) claim that the principles of the socio-cultural theory (SCT) can also apply to second language acquisition. They explain that "SCT is grounded in a perspective that does not separate the individual from the social context and in fact argues that the individual emerges from social interaction and as such is always fundamentally a social being" (pp. 217–218). Menezes (2008) adds that it is in the social world that language learners observe others using language and imitate them. It is also with the collaboration of other social actors that learners move from one stage to another.

One of the main concepts proposed by Vygotsky (1934/1978) is the Zone of Proximal Development (ZPD), which is understood as the assistance one learner receives from another person, a 'knowledgeable other' (e.g. parents, caregivers, relatives, teachers, classmates), which enables the learner to perform a learning task. The Communicative Approach focuses on cultural and social aspects that play a significant role in students acquiring and learning a foreign/second language.

Finocchiaro and Brumfit (1983) provide several distinctive characteristics of the Communicative Approach such as: dialogs center around communicative functions, and are not memorized. Contextualization is a basic premise and learning language is learning to communicate. Effective communication and comprehensive pronunciation are sought, and attempts to communicate may be encouraged from the very beginning of the language learning process. The target linguistic system is learned best through the process of struggling to communicate, and communicative competence is the desired goal. Communicative competence is defined not only as an inherent grammatical competence but also as the ability to use competent grammar in numerous communicative situations (Hymes, 1972). Students are expected to interact with each other either face-to-face or through writing, and intrinsic motivation will spring from an interest in what is being communicated (Finocchiaro & Brumfit, 1983).

Richards and Rogers (2014) summing up the fundamental principles of the Communicative Approach say that EFL and ESL students learn a language through authentic and meaningful communication, as the goal of classroom activities. Learning is a process of creative construction and involves trial and error. Communication involves the integration of different language skills. Fluency is an important characteristic of communication.

According to the Silent Way method of the Communicative Approach, learners are supposed to be observers and then be able to describe situations in the target language, focusing especially on the actions they were able to see (Herrera & Murry, 2011). The native language of learners is not used. The teacher focuses instead on the students' pronunciation and encourages the development of speaking skills. The teacher is silent at the beginning of the students' learning process, allowing students to be autonomous and independent, to take initiative, and to promote language interaction (Gattegno, 1982).

In other words, one of the teachers' tasks is to monitor students' interaction, so that they are helpful and do not interfere with students' learning (Larsen-Freeman, 2011).

Another method of the Communicative Approach is the Natural Way, which according to Richards and Rogers (2014), focuses on comprehension and meaningful communication as well as the provision of the right kinds of comprehensible input, to provide the necessary and sufficient conditions for successful classroom foreign and second language acquisition. The originality of the Natural Way lies in the fact that it emphasizes comprehensible and meaningful practice activities, rather than production of grammatically perfect utterances and sentences.

An important component of the Communicative Approach is based on learning a language where students' personalities are of more importance than their intellect (Herrera & Murry, 2011), and what could be learned intuitively and spontaneously, as opposed to being aware of the grammatical rules of a foreign/second language. Therefore, a relaxing, low anxiety, and risk-free environment (created, for example through playing music in the background) is of significant importance when learning a language, which could enhance language acquisition (Lozanov, 1982). Students work with text first in their native language, then in the target language through visual aids supporting the meaning of the text, and through conversations, retellings, and role-playing. Activities such as games, songs and gymnastic exercises are also included (Bancroft, 1972).

Therefore, in order to enhance students' success, the following suggestions are advisable: seeking out and structuring opportunities for the use of the target language in interpersonal communications; attention to the needs, desires, interests, and individual aspirations of students; acceptance without constant corrections of all attempts at target language production; and accepting of the use of students' native languages in the classroom. Teachers should also scaffold their instruction through hands-on activities, social interaction, cooperative learning, guided vocabulary, and visual support such as images, objects, manipulatives, and realia (Herrera & Murry, 2011). There is also an emphasis on the importance of context in foreign/second language acquisition through the use of photos, drawings, charts, and diagrams (Kelly, 1976).

Link between the Study, the Communicative Approach and its Methodology

My study is related to the Communicative Approach and its methodology, as it discusses the role of environment in learning, including students learning from each other. I was interested in how Polish teachers create a classroom environment and what teaching methodology they expose their students to, so they can learn from each other; e.g., in pair/group activities to develop their speaking, communicative, and cooperative skills in the English language.

Research demonstrates that despite the common acceptance of communicative teaching of language, it has been challenging in EFL countries (Li, 1998). Therefore, I was curious how the Polish EFL teachers mediate and filter the communicative teaching-learning process to make it suitable for the local Polish culture and environment, where EFL students are not exposed to developing their communicative skills outside of the classroom, as daily communication in Poland takes place in the Polish language on a daily basis.

Cognitive Approach

The Cognitive Approach is a result of examining and analyzing the cognitive psychological side of learning, language learning and teaching, thus students learn a foreign/second language (O'Malley & Chamot, 1990). Cognitive psychology is concerned with the structure and nature of knowledge processes such as discovering, recognizing, judging, reasoning, reflecting, and their influences on relationships to actions (Elman et al., 1997; Gagné et al., 1993; Shuell, 1986). In teaching-learning languages the Cognitive Approach is associated particularly with the elaboration on prior knowledge, note-taking, deduction/induction, resourcing, grouping, summarizing, imagery, auditory representation, and making inferences (Herrera & Murry, 2011).

The most crucial method in the Cognitive Approach is CALLA (Cognitive Academic Language Learning Approach). As mentioned by the Colorado Department of Education (2011), CALLA was designed to provide comprehensible instruction for English Language Learners (ELLs) in ESL or bilingual programs. CALLA integrates language development, content area instruction, and explicit instruction in learning strategies. In CALLA, content is the main focus in the teaching-learning process, and academic language skills can be developed as the need for them emerges from the content (Colorado Department of Education, 2011). So how does CALLA work?

> Through a comprehensive lesson plan based on cognitive theory and efforts to integrate academic language and learning strategies with content, CALLA lessons rely on content to determine the academic language selections and learning strategies to be taught and these lessons rely heavily on scaffolding, or the provision of instructional supports when concepts and skills are first introduced and the gradual removal of

supports as students develop greater proficiency, knowledge, and skills. (Colorado Department of Education, 2011, p. 2)

CALLA also includes such components as: valuing students' prior knowledge and cultural experience, relating this knowledge to academic learning in a new language and culture; developing language awareness and critical literacy; social interaction and successful working with others; learning through cooperative learning tasks; and evaluating students' own learning and planning how to become more effective and independent learners (Herrera & Murry, 2011).

Link between This Study, the Cognitive Approach and its Methodology

My study is related to the Cognitive Approach and its methodology because, the Cognitive Approach emphasizes the importance of students' background, communication, group work, hands-on experiences, inquiry-based, and cooperative learning, which play an important role in the process of teaching and learning.

In examining the development of Polish students' speaking, communicative, and cooperative skills in the English language through their teachers, I was interested in the activities EFL teachers in Poland engage in with their students. I wondered if the students have opportunities to have hands-on experiences, learn how to communicate, negotiate meaning, and cooperate to create group projects. I was also eager to learn how teachers connect the content knowledge with students' prior knowledge and experience, and what tools the teachers in Poland use in the classroom to enhance their students' process of learning English, especially when it comes to verbal language production and the development of cooperative skills in EFL.

Summary of the Three Teaching Approaches

I reviewed the three EFL and ESL approaches and methodologies. The Grammatical/Grammar-Based Approach is connected with the traditional way of teaching language the study participants and I grew up in. The Communicative and the Cooperative Approaches and their methodologies are relevant to my study, as they are connected with the development of speaking, communicative, and cooperative skills in students by their teachers, which my study focused on. Communication, dialog, interaction, role play, student-centered instruction, and active learning lie in the core of developing students' speaking, communicative, and cooperative skills in English. My intention was to connect the above approaches and their methodologies through my hands-on experience, such as actual observations and interviews of EFL teachers I conducted in Poland.

I also realize that the development of speaking, communicative, and cooperative skills in students is a dynamic and fluid process and cannot be exactly pinned to a particular EFL and ESL approach and a teaching-learning methodology. Some teachers decide on a single approach or/and method, some take certain aspects from different approaches and/or methodologies and incorporate them into their teaching in the form of activities/techniques and other practices. However, my hope was to see the presence and application of FLA/SLA approaches and methodologies to some degree reflected in the limited environment of the Polish classroom, through teaching practices, contributing to the development of Polish students' English speaking, communicative, and cooperative skills.

The sociocultural reality of Poland significantly differs from the sociocultural reality of English-speaking countries, where ESL students have the advantage to learn the English language in its natural environment. However, all the EFL and ESL approaches and methodologies are applicable to every country, not only where ESL acquisition and learning takes place, but also where EFL occurs, especially in the era of advanced technology where the environment of the second language acquisition and learning can be simulated electronically by EFL teachers for their students.

So far I have discussed the three approaches to teaching a foreign/second language. There are other aspects of teaching EFL in Poland, which I was interested in exploring while conducting my research and these are: process of democratization of education in Poland, the use of technology by Polish EFL teachers, student-centered instruction, and teaching and learning in an authentic environment.

Process of Democratization of Education in Poland

During the intervening years, times and culture have changed. As pointed out by Bogaj et al. (1999), "The political transformation in Poland opened an entirely new perspective of social development" (p. 13). Poland is not behind the "Iron Curtain" anymore. The country's borders opened, and Poland became a member of the European Union in 2004 (Thompson, 2004). As mentioned by Dąbrowski and Wiśniewski (2011), in the last 20 years Poland has gone through a major transition process in which the challenges for education in terms of new approaches to teaching and learning have been accompanied by vast changes such as the democratization of political, societal, economic, cultural and educational structures, and processes.

The process was prompted by the fall of communism in Poland, open borders between Poland and the Anglo (native English-speaking) countries, especially Great Britain and the United States, as more methodological materials became accessible from the countries for the EFL teachers and their students in Poland. Also, the materials were travelling faster thanks to more and more available technology, which promoted student-centered and hands-on EFL methodology, focused on the development of students' speaking, communicative, and cooperative skills in Polish schools and English language institutions. Since the early 1990s the Polish educational system has undergone a complex series of reforms, many of which were simultaneous. There had been significant shifts in the learning and teaching process brought about by numerous international influences. Dąbrowski and Wiśniewski (2011) mention:

> Parents' expectations have evolved and students are growing up in a much more connected environment with the Internet and social networks and an exponential development of access to ICT and the need for digital competences and a range of key competences for lifelong learning and work. (p. 323)

The process of learning and teaching EFL in Poland became influenced, in particular, by various student-centered, communicative, and cooperative teaching approaches, which came from native English-speaking countries such as Great Britain and the United States.

Today, every student in Poland desires and is expected to learn English. Students start learning English as early as the first grade of elementary school through middle, and high school, as well as into college. In numerous cases, children start learning English even in kindergarten, as mentioned by my brother, a father of two small children residing permanently in Poland. Therefore, "...some parents send their young to English-language pre-schools although few of them exist" (Reichelt, 2005, p. 223).

Some students are motivated to learn English because it is required in almost every job. Poland's borders are open, thus Polish citizens can travel abroad, and the language of communication in many other countries is English. Poland's European Union membership and access to jobs that do not require work permits in other European Union countries motivated many Polish residents to immigrate to Great Britain and Ireland searching for better economic opportunities, as the unemployment rate in Poland is above 10 percent (Trading Economics, 2015). According to O'Farrell (2005), 33,000 Polish workers have arrived in Ireland since Poland's accession to the European Union in May, 2004. Due to this and similar situations, it is recommended by the European Council that every European citizen ought to know at least two other languages apart from their native language (European Council, 2002).

Many of Polish EFL students realize the necessity of possessing speaking, communicative, and cooperative skills required for future jobs. After the fall of communism many western foreign investors from such countries as Germany, Holland, Italy, France and Great Britain look for cheaper labor and have been bringing their businesses to Poland and employing local employees. In order for the employers and employees to communicate, knowledge of the English language is expected of both of the parties. Hence, Polish students and future employees develop their speaking, communicative, and cooperative skills in English by attending evening English courses or attending sessions with private tutors (Lekki, 2003). As reported by 2003 data, 80 percent of high school students were learning English (Education across Europe, 2003). While students get free public school education, their parents pay substantial sums of money to develop their children's English language in private institutions and places outside of school. Teaching English is a booming business in Poland. During communism tutoring was mainly conducted at teachers' homes. After the fall of communism in 1989 (Odrowaz, 2009), numerous English language schools legally and openly mushroomed all over the country, especially in cities and towns. The state has been supporting foreign language education in public education ever since by providing financial support for the schools with a particular goal of investing money and resources to support youth's development of knowledge and skills, especially English.

The Use of Technology in Instruction

Youth have a strong interest in technology, and it also continues to be popular in teaching and learning (Blair, 2012). Incorporation of technological tools such as computers, audio and video cameras, software, and overhead projectors, make the teaching and learning experience more interesting, powerful, and richer. Research shows that the use of technology motivates EFL and ESL learners (Traore & Kyei-Blankson, 2011). It also acts as "...a stimulus for language development" (Butler-Pascoe & Wiburg, 2003, p. 84). Through the use of technology, teachers have an ability to create a student-friendly, non-threatening environment and a safe space where students can feel free to take risks and be engaged in new learning so they can develop their critical thinking abilities and feel free to share their ideas, opinions, and thoughts.

Computers combine voice, image, color, and motion, activating students' senses, which help to enhance their language skills. For example, they visually can remember new vocabulary and pronunciation of new words, etc. Butler-Pascoe and Wiburg (2003) state, "Computers allow teachers to add multi-sensory elements, text, sound, picture, video, and animation, which provide meaningful contexts to facilitate comprehension" (p. 84). Computers are also of a nonjudgmental in nature, and they provide students with the ability to review materials numerous times without being exposed to embarrassment, fear, and anxiety, and they can change the new learning into comprehensive input (Butler-Pascoe & Wiburg, 2003).

Computers also promote communication and cooperation among EFL and ESL students if they are assigned to perform a group activity. As Bowman and Plaisir (1996) say, "Teamwork is essential to the success of the projects and student realize that they must work together if they are to complete the activities" (p. 27). As Freire (2000) mentions, "I've no doubt about the enormous potential for technology to motivate and challenge children and adolescents..." (p. 82).

Student-Centered Instruction

How can a teacher create conditions for student-centered instruction without giving up her/his control in the class? It can be accomplished by sharing the teaching-learning process with students, as "Student-centered instruction is a form of active learning where students are engaged in what they are studying" (Brown, 2008, p. 30). Brooks and Brooks (2000) advise asking questions and directing students to solutions rather than just providing answers. They maintain to keep the goal in mind of feeding students with natural curiosity. Brown (2008) recommends that, "...the teacher becomes a coach, or instigator, who is always there to assist, but never to give away answers" (p. 33).

This concept of student-centered instruction was for the first time introduced by the American educator John Dewey and the Russian psychologist Lev Vygotsky about 115 years ago. Dewey (1897/2011), so revolutionary for his times stated the teacher should not be one to stand at the front of the room doling out bits of information to be absorbed by passive students. Dewey (1916/1963) pointed out as well that students learn more by doing and experiencing than by only observing.

Student-centered instruction includes providing opportunities for students to interact with each other (Peyton et al., 2010). Vygotsky (1934/1978), ahead of his time, also emphasized the importance of interpersonal communication and social interaction with a skillful tutor in the process of learning and Menezes (2008) highlights that based on Vygotskian thoughts, language learning is a socially mediated process. Scaffolding is also a significant feature of CALLA, the previously mentioned Cognitive Approach teaching method, where "...lessons rely heavily on scaffolding, or the provision of instructional supports when concepts and skills are first introduced and the gradual removal of supports as students develop greater proficiency, knowledge, and skills" (Colorado Department of Education, 2011, p. 2). As Herrera and Murry (2011) point out, teachers scaffold their instruction through hands-on activities, social interaction, cooperative learning and visual support such as images, object manipulatives and realia (artifacts from places where students live and work).

Larsen-Freeman (2011) adds that one of the teachers' tasks is to monitor student interactions, so that they are helpful and do not interfere with student learning. The interaction usually takes place in the form of pair work and small groups. There is classroom based research that supports the notion that language learning is facilitated through opportunities for students to interact with each other in small groups or in pairs (Hellermann, 2007; Morris & Tarone, 2003).

Students need to see the purpose of their learning, and the process needs to be meaningful to them. As mentioned by McCombs and Whisler (1997), learning is most meaningful when topics and class themes can be applied to students' interests, educational needs, and lives in general. This can be done by facilitating student work in pairs, in groups, or alone, depending on the purpose of the activity, and creating learning opportunities that mirror actual tasks in students' lives (Bell, 2004; Ellis, 2009). Peyton et al. (2010) add that student-centered approaches seek to engage students actively in learning in ways that are appropriate for and relevant to them in their lives outside the classroom.

In student-centered teaching, the creation of a student-friendly class atmosphere and environment is crucial for students to be successful learners. This concept is pointed out by Lozanov (1982) who says that a relaxing, low anxiety, and risk-free environment is of significant importance in learning a language, which can enhance language acquisition. Krashen, as quoted in Herrera and Murry (2011), also talks about the importance of a student-friendly environment in the process of learning a language. Krashen developed the hypothesis of effective filter, which is a 'screen' that is influenced by emotional variables that can prevent learning. According to Krashen, the affective filter can be triggered by various mind states, such as anxiety, self-confidence, motivation and stress. The higher the effective filter, the worse are the conditions for students to acquire and learn a target language.

Teaching and Learning in an Authentic Environment

In student-centered teaching, the importance of a student-friendly classroom environment creation is emphasized, as it promotes the development of EFL and ESL. However, as the classroom environment is concerned, it is also crucial to create the authentic language environment.

Learning English as a Foreign Language is challenging, and students in non-English speaking countries are in a disadvantaged position because foreign language learners in these countries "...have little or no exposure to the second [and foreign] language outside the classroom" (Seliger, 1988, p. 27). In other words, EFL learners lack the social and cultural context of the English language, unlike their ESL peers living in English-speaking countries. Hence, EFL learners by the nature of their geographical location, do not receive an equal opportunity to reach the same level of achievement as ESL learners living in an English-speaking country, who are exposed to the English language on everyday basis all the time. Brown (2014) declares that few if any people achieve fluency in a foreign language solely within the confines of the classroom (p. 1). Therefore, there is urgency among teachers of EFL to find creative ways to be able to enhance their EFL students' abilities to learn English as close to the fluency of native speakers of English as it is humanly possible.

Even though EFL students have limited access English, they do not live in a vacuum; they have an opportunity to read press and publications in English, watch English language television, and surf the Internet. They learn a basic understanding of the world around them, about the political, economic, and social perspectives. Students also subconsciously perform various social roles, such as an online customer, an applicant, an email writer, a caller, and so forth. Therefore, what teachers of English need to do is not only teach the English language per se but also teach students how to use English in society, regardless if it is in the foreign language environment or the native language environment (Krukiewicz-Gacek et al., 2007). Consequently, learners need to make connections between the language and content they are learning in class and their own realities in the world (Coatney, 2006). The topics include family, raising children, and communicating effectively (Weinstein, 1999). The importance of providing opportunities for meaningful interaction and connecting instruction to learners' lives outside the classroom is highlighted in many professional development materials (e.g., Celce-Murcía, 2001; National Center for Family Literacy and Center for Applied Linguistics, 2008).

One of the ways to create a more authentic classroom environment is to use authentic materials in English classes, which Harmer (1991), cited in Matsuta (n.d., p. 1), defines as materials and texts as those that are meant for native speakers of English and not for English language students. Jordan (1997) refers to authentic texts as "...texts that are not written for language teaching purposes" (p. 113). Authentic materials are significant since they increase students' motivation for learning, and expose learner to the 'real' language (Guariento & Morley, 2001, p. 347). The use of authentic materials in the classroom is exciting for both, the teachers and the students. Chavez (1998) mentions that learners enjoy dealing with authentic materials as they enable them to interact with real language and its use. Kilickaya (2004) confirms:

> They [authentic materials] have a positive effect on learner motivation, deliver authentic cultural information, provide exposure to real language, are related more closely to learners' needs and they support a more creative approach to teaching and learning. We can claim that learners are being exposed to real language and they feel that they are learning the 'real' language. These are what make us excited and willing to use authentic materials in our classrooms.... (p. 2)

The main advantages of using authentic materials are:
- They provide real cultural information.
- They provide access to the native English language.
- They have a positive effect on students' motivation.
- They are more associated with students' needs.
- They support a more creative approach to teaching and learning (Philips & Shettlesworth, 1978; Clarke, 1989; Peacock, 1997, as cited in Richards, 2001).

Summary

Chapter 2 overviews three main teaching a foreign/second language approaches and demonstrated how they are connected with the research conducted in a public high school in Poland involving interviews and classroom observations of five participating Polish EFL teachers. This chapter also concentrates on other aspects of the teaching-learning dynamic, such as: a process of democratization in Poland, the use of technology in the classroom, student-centered instruction, and authentic teaching-learning. In my research I looked for the presence of the themes and how they were connected with the five research participants in their own journeys of learning the English language and how they were used in the classroom, with a particular focus on the ways the participants developed their students' speaking, communicative, and cooperative skills in English.

In Chapter 3, I present the methodology I used in doing this research. I explain the research paradigm and research approach. I also describe the five participants, the research setting, the instrumentations, how and when the data was collected, analyzed, what the purpose, significance and need of the study were. I explain the research design and research procedure. I also demonstrate issues associated with validity of the study, the dissertation committee's involvement, and what the role the five participants played in writing this study.

Methods

Introduction

In Chapter 1, I described the historical overview of teaching and learning English in Poland before communism, and how the resulting political, social, cultural, economic, and educational transformations led to the change of teaching English these days. In Chapter 2, I summarized three main teaching a foreign/second language approaches and presented how they were associated with my research conducted at a high school in Poland. Chapter 2 also focused on other aspects of the teaching-learning process such as a process of democratization in Poland, the use of technology, student-centered instruction, and authentic teaching-learning. In my research, I searched for the presence of the themes and how they were associated with my five participants personally on their paths of learning English in Poland. I also examined how they were utilized in the five participants' classrooms, with an emphasis on the ways the participants developed their students' communicative, cooperative, and speaking skills in the English language. In Chapter 3, I discuss the methodology I used in conducting my research.

With recommendations by my Dissertation Co-chairs and Committee Members, and with permission for doing the research granted by the Institution Review Board (IRB) at New Mexico State University, I moved to southern Poland for three months, from February 15 to May 15, 2015. During this time, I observed and interviewed five Polish EFL high school teachers to examine the ways they manifested their pedagogical practices in order to develop their Polish students' speaking, communicative, and cooperative skills in English in school. I used a qualitative research paradigm and a case study method. In order to understand what it means that my research is of qualitative nature, it is important to explain how scholars define qualitative research.

Joubish et al. (2011) say qualitative research seeks out the 'why,' not the 'how' of its topic through the analysis of unstructured information – things like unstructured interview transcripts, open ended survey responses, emails, notes, feedback forms, photos, and videos. Qualitative research is used to gain insight into people's attitudes, behaviors, value systems, concerns, motivations, aspirations, culture or lifestyle, and it helps us understand how people feel and why they feel as they do. Qualitative research is concerned with developing explanations of social phenomena. Therefore, its aim is to help us understand the world in which we live and why things are the way they are (Joubish et al., 2011).

© KONINKLIJKE BRILL NV, LEIDEN, 2019 | DOI:10.1163/9789004394377_003

Purpose of the Study

My purpose of this study was to observe and interview five participating teachers and learn what their paths were in becoming EFL teachers and to examine how they teach EFL today with a focus on developing their students' speaking, communicative, and cooperative skills. I was also interested in how the teaching of English changed from the communist era to the current period.

My intention was also to observe and examine how EFL high school instructors in Poland teach their students and share my research findings with other members in the EFL field so they will be able to take into consideration and incorporate my research and enhance and enrich in this way their teaching-learning methodology in their institutions and communities.

Denzin and Lincoln (2005) point out that "...qualitative research consists of a set of interpretive, material practices that turn the world into a series of representations, including field notes, interviews, conversations, photographs, recordings and memos to the self" (p. 3). Eisenhardt (1989) adds that "...interviews, observations, and archival sources are particularly common..." (p. 537).

Therefore, using the qualitative design and case study approach of research, my study was guided to analyze factors leading to high school teachers' developing their students' speaking, communicative, and cooperative skills in English. I did this by observing, interviewing, and examining the daily teaching routines of five Polish EFL high school teachers who educate their students on all levels of English: beginning, intermediate, and advanced. I used two different data collection instruments: class observations, and interviews, as only a mixture of various instruments of data collection can be the most effective when conducting a classroom oriented study (Nunan, 1992).

Research Design

My research was conducted in the context of educational changes influenced by political, educational, cultural, economic, and social changes in the last twenty-five years in Poland. Denzin and Lincoln (2005) say that qualitative research involves an interpretive, naturalistic approach to the world and that researchers study things in their natural settings, attempting to make sense of, or interpret phenomena in terms of the meanings people bring to them. Creswell (2007) adds that qualitative researchers tend to collect data in the field at the site where participants experience the issue or problem under study; researchers do not bring individuals into a lab.

Therefore, my research was conveyed in multiple locations with multiple participants in multiple situations to establish the connection between the educational and political changes and the development of students' speaking, communicative, and cooperative skills in the English language.

I selected a case study approach for this research, which Eisenhardt (1989) describes as:

> ...a research strategy, which focuses on understanding the dynamics present within single settings.... Case studies typically combine data collection methods such as archives, interviews, questionnaires, and observations.... The evidence may be qualitative (e.g., words), quantitative (e.g., numbers), or both. (pp. 533–534)

In this case study, the evidence researched is qualitative data. Ultimately, case studies can be used to accomplish different goals: to provide a description (Kidder, 1982), to test a theory (Pinfield, 1986; Anderson, 1983), and/or to generate a theory (e.g., Gersick, 1988; Harris & Sutton, 1986). In this case study research, it is providing a description.

Thus, this qualitative case study researched five EFL public high school teachers in Poland, considered their stories of learning English, and examined the ways they manifest their pedagogical practices to develop and enhance their students' speaking, communicative, and cooperative skills in the English language. The overarching question for the research is: How do five EFL teachers in Poland manifest their pedagogical practices? This general research question also contained several sub-questions.

Sub-question 1) What kinds of experience and educational preparation do the five Polish EFL teachers have?

Sub-question 2) How do Polish EFL teachers describe their EFL methodologies as related to their students' speaking, communicative, and cooperative skills, and how is their philosophy manifested in a classroom setting?

Sub-question 3a) How do these EFL teachers reflect on teaching practices prior to and subsequent to the fall of communism?

Sub-question 3b) Given that there are social, economic, and pedagogical differences in EFL pre- and post-communism, what evidence do the teachers provide that their practices in teaching EFL have changed over time?

Description of the Participants

I ensured there were at least five participants who were able to complete this study as advised by Creswell (2007), "Typically...the researcher chooses no less than four or five cases," which gives the researcher a sense of "generalizability" (p. 76).

The research participants were recruited through an acquaintance of mine, who is a public school teacher, residing in the same southern Poland city as the participants do. On my behalf, the acquaintance asked for volunteers in one of the public high schools, who were teaching EFL that were willing to participate in my study. On July 8, 2014 the principal of the school granted me a permission to conduct observations and hold interviews with teachers from her institution.

The research participants were EFL high school teachers whom I had never met prior and with whom I had not previously communicated. All of the teachers were women between ages 32 and 47, and came from one public high school in southern Poland. The reason I selected these participants whom I had no personal or professional connection with was because I desired to ensure objective and fresh perspective about high school English education in Poland at present. In my opinion, observing and interviewing participants who were previously unknown to me gave me the sense of a higher objectivity.

"The selection of participants is neither necessary, nor even preferable;" therefore for this study, "...the sample was not random, but reflected the selection of specific cases" (Eisenhardt, 1989, p. 537). Consequently, the participants in this study represented a purposeful sample. Schatzman and Strauss (1973) state that purposeful sampling is a practical necessity that is "...shaped by the time the researcher has available to him, by his framework, by his starting and developing interests, and by any restrictions placed upon his observations by his hosts" (p. 39). Purposeful sampling participants are those who have more specific information and particular knowledge related to the study (Coyne, 1997). Therefore, four of the participants in my study had an extensive teaching experience, reaching back to the communist era, and the other remaining participant had teaching experience in the post-communist era. They all were observed and interviewed during their daily teaching routines in the spring 2015 semester, from the middle of February to the middle of May. The participants were told to conduct their classes as they normally would and not to make any adjustments because of the research.

Instrumentation

The instrumentation used in this study included observations and interviews.

Observations

Observation is "...the systematic description of events, behaviors, and arti-facts in the social setting chosen for study" (Marshall & Rossman, 1989, p. 79). Observations empower the researcher to depict enduring situations using the five senses, providing a "written photograph" of the situation under study (Erlandson et al., 1993). Participant observation according to Kawulich (2005), is the process of making researchers able to learn about the actions, such that learning is achieved "...of the research participants in the natural environment through observing and participating in those actions, such that learning is achieved "...through exposure to or involvement in the day-to-day or routine activities of participants in the researcher setting" (Schensul et al., 1999, p. 91).

During my observations (recorded through hard copy notes only) in line with the above observation definitions, I was looking for specific information concerning the ways a given participant was working with her students in order to develop their speaking, communicative, and cooperative skills. The participants were not asked to act any differently during the observations, and I was selective in taking notes during the observations. For example, when a given participant was working on developing her students' listening and writ-ing skills, the information was typically not recorded in my notes and is not included in this dissertation either.

The observations took place in the school where the participants worked as EFL teachers. Between February and May, 2015, I attended the participants' classes and observed them while they were teaching. Each observation lasted approximately 45 minutes, and there were at least three, four observations of each of the participants per week. All the observations were scheduled with the participants in advance. The fact that I was present face-to face in the observed classes enabled me to take hard copy notes on a regular basis. At all times I tried to keep a low profile, and I made the effort I was not to be an obstruction to regular class dynamics and routines, therefore, I was always sit-ting at the back of a classroom. The data obtained from the observations and hard copy notes were developed on a daily basis while they were still fresh in my mind and then recorded in my computer.

Interviews

In addition to observations, I also conducted interviews, which Dexter (2006), Hayman et al. (1954), and Mishler (1986) define as both a research methodology and a social relationship that must be nurtured, sustained, and then gracefully ended. The participants in my study were asked to complete a 180-minute-long in-depth interview divided into three parts, each about 60 minutes long, over the course of three weeks. The concept of the three interviews was based on

Seidman's (2013) approach towards interviews. He suggests the following structure for the interviews: "The first interview establishes the context of the participants' experience. The second allows participants to reconstruct the details
of their experience within the context in which it occurs. And the third encourages the participants to reflect on the meaning their experience holds for them"
(p. 21). Seidman (2013), explaining also the purpose of the interviews, says:

> In the first interview, the interviewer's task is to put the participant's
> experience in context by asking him or her to tell as much as possible
> about him or herself in light of the topic up to the present time.... The
> purpose of the second interview is to concentrate on the concrete details
> of the participants' present lived experience in the topic area of the study.
> We ask them to reconstruct the details.... In the third interview, we ask
> participants to reflect on the meaning of their experience. The question
> of "meaning" is not one of satisfaction or reward, although such issues
> may play a part in the participants' thinking. Rather, it addresses intel-
> lectual and emotional connections between the participants work and
> life. (pp. 21–22)

The concept of three interviews per participants in my research was based on
Irving Seidman's understanding in-depth interviews, however I adapted his
concept to the need of my research. Therefore, the interviews in my research
were 60 minutes-long as opposed to 90 minutes-long. Also, it was my idea to
call the three interviews in my study as: historical, contemporary, and reflective. My interview questions were as follows:

In the *first part* of the interview, which I called *historical*, the five participants recounted their past experiences as students and teachers of English. In
the *second part* of the interview, which I called *contemporary*, the participants
were asked to describe how they taught to promote the speaking, communicative, and cooperative skills of their students. In the *third part* of the interview,
which I called *reflective* (while keeping in mind the answers to the participants'
first two questions), they were asked to reflect on their teaching practices in
association with developing their students' speaking, communicative, and
cooperative skills.

Research Procedure

At the first meeting with each of the research participants, the consent form
was presented. I went over the form with each of the five participants and

asked if all the information was understood by each of them. After presenting the consent form to the participants, going over it and answering their questions, each of the potential participants was asked to sign the consent form, which they did.

Their participation in my research was completely voluntary. The research participants were free to refuse to take part in the project or to leave the research project at any time if they became uncomfortable. They were allowed to decline to answer any questions and were free to stop taking part in the project at any time. Whether or not they chose to participate in the research and whether or not they chose to answer questions or continue participating in the project, there was no penalty to them or loss of benefits to which they were otherwise entitled. The participants were also assured that there would be no foreseen physical, psychological, emotional, social, economic, or spiritual risks associated with the completion of this study.

There were no direct interviews with the students. The purpose of this study was to see how the teachers, not the students, facilitated student learning in the classroom. Student participation in the research was completely voluntary as well. If the parents or the student did not wish to participate in the study the student was allowed to work elsewhere during the observations. The students were free to refuse to take part in the study. They were able to decline to answer any questions and were free to stop taking part in the study at any time. During the observations, as mentioned above, the researcher only used hard copy notes in the form of field notes. No audio, video or camera recorders were used in the classrooms either.

Data Collection

I started observing and interviewing the five participants in the middle of February and continued until the middle of May 2015. During the data collection I paid close attention to the five participants to be able to observe their ideas, thoughts, feelings, gestures, and actions as they related to the study in order to understand the phenomenon under investigation (Creswell, 2007; Seidman, 2013). The observations took place in the school environment, and I had no opportunity to observe the five participants in their social context outside of the school environment. During the observations I had a separate note book for each of the five participants.

Data Analysis

Each of the five participants had a separate folder, which I color-coded. I created a profile of each of the participants, which allowed me "...to present the participant in context, to clarify his or her intentions, and convey a sense of process and time, all central components of qualitative analysis" (Seidman, 2013, p. 122). Then I looked for commonalities in the participants' answers that informed my research. My role in the study was of an observer, a describer, and an analyzer, without passing any judgments on the ways the five participants I interviewed were developing their students' speaking, communicative, and cooperative skills.

Through data collection and data analysis I produced the report on classroom observations, which was written in a narrative form. I put the information into categories, recognized commonalities, analyzed emerging themes, and drew conclusions. However, I concentrated on documenting and on describing, and not on judging in the categories of failure or success, as my aim was to report observations, and interviews to demonstrate the matter within a case analysis (Merriam, 1991). The participants and other people familiarized with this study were able to enhance their knowledge of meaning through lessons learned from this research (Lincoln & Guba, 1985). In order words, the participants were able to reflect on their experiences, feelings, and practices, and what these meant to them.

All of the data provided by the research participants (in the form of hard copy notes, digital recordings and their transcriptions), and the analysis conducted by myself, was kept confidential and anonymous in a locked cabinet located at my home. The five participants' names were not associated with the data that was collected from them. Instead, they were given pseudonyms, in order to keep their data completely confidential and anonymous. My research supervisors and I are the only persons who had access to the data collected during this study. The results from the study could be used in degree seeking research, reports, publications and presentations, however – the participants' identities would not be included in any of these. They will remain anonymous and each of the five participants received a fictional first name.

The data will be kept for five years from the time the research began: February 15, 2015. After that time, the digital data will be permanently erased from my digital recorder and my personal computer. The hard copy data will be shredded and the digital data will be permanently deleted. Thus, the hard copy data and the digital data will be destroyed on February 14, 2020.

Validity of the Study

Qualitative research, unlike quantitative research, rarely has the benefit of formal comparison, sampling strategies, or statistical manipulations that "control
for" the effect of particular variables, and qualitative researchers must try to
rule out most validity threats after the research has begun by using evidence
collected during the research itself (Maxwell, 2008). Maxwell (2008) considers
two types of threats in qualitative research: *bias*, defined as "...ways in which
data collection or analysis are distorted by the researcher's theory, values, or
preconceptions" (p. 243) and *reactivity*, defined as "trying to "control for" the
effect of the researcher..." (p. 242).

In order to have validity in my research I concentrated on Maxwell's
(2008) three validity suggestions: *intensive long-term involvement, "rich"
data,* and *respondent validation.* Intensive, long-term participant observation (involvement), as claimed by Becker and Geer (1957), provides more
complete data about specific situations and events than any other method.
Therefore, I observed my participants every day for three months and conducted three in-depth 180-minute-long interviews with the participants.
"Rich" data, as pointed out by Becker (1970), is data that is detailed and
varied enough to provide a full and revealing picture of what is going on.
On the recommendation of Maxwell, in order to obtain "rich" data I did
verbatim transcripts of the interviews, not just notes on what I felt was
significant.

Respondent validation (Bryman, 1988; Lincoln & Guba, 1985), refers to as
member checks and define as "...systematically soliciting feedback about
one's data and conclusions from the people you are studying" (Maxwell, 2008,
p. 244). Therefore, I was in communication with my participants and available for feedback in person, by e-mail and phone to "...rule out the possibility of misinterpreting the meaning of what participants say and do and the
perspective they have on what is going on, as well as being an important way
of identifying your own biases and misunderstandings of what you observed"
(Maxwell, 2008, p. 244).

In my study each of the five research participants obtained a copy of the
complete dissertation and was asked to read the whole dissertation and provide feedback, where they could clarify, provide additional information, or
delete material. All the participants complied with the request. My intention is to have the final published at some point in the future. I asked the
professors to read the dissertation in its entirety, so they had a full view of
what I did.

Summary

This chapter described the research methodology, data collection and data analysis I used to answer my research question. The chapter also described the main participants (teachers) and secondary participants (students). Precautions to ensure the participants' privacy, anonymity, and rights were described briefly in this chapter and the participant consent forms was attached to this research in the Appendix section.

This chapter also connects my methodology with qualitative research literature represented by scholars such as: Yvonne S. Lincoln, Egon G. Guba, John W. Creswell, Joseph A. Maxwell, Irving Seidman, and others. After collecting data for my research, I organized the information into categories to discover commonalities between and among the participants, analyzed emerging themes, and reached conclusions.

Findings

Introduction

In Chapter 4, I described the historical overview of teaching and learning English in Poland before communism and how the political, social and educational transformations led to the change of teaching English these days. In Chapter 2, I highlighted three teaching a foreign/second language approaches, and presented how they were associated with my research. I also highlighted other aspects of the teaching-learning process, which were: a process of democratization in Poland, the use of technology, student-centered instruction and authentic teaching-learning. In my research I searched for the presence of the themes and how they were associated with my five participants personally in their journey of learning English in Poland, and also how the themes were utilized in the participants' classrooms with an emphasis on the ways they developed speaking, communicative, and cooperative skills in their EFL students.

In Chapter 3, I discussed the methodology I used in conducting the research, and how I incorporated such aspects as: purpose of the study, research design, questions asked, instrumentation, research procedure, data collection, data analysis, validity of the study, and working with the Dissertation Committee.

In Chapter 4, I explore the ways the five participating teachers learned English as students and how their ways of learning about political, technological, social and educational changes led to the ways the participants teach English to their students now focusing on the students' speaking, communicative, and cooperative skills.

The Site of the Study

The school the study took place in is located in a southern Poland city. It is one of the two most prestigious high schools in the city. The school has very high standards and expectations and all students are required to learn English and another foreign language. Among these, after English, German is the most popular. Students go to high school for three years. They attend content-based classes in cohorts. However, as far as English is concerned they are grouped according to their levels of proficiency. In the last grade, they are expected to take a language exam (usually English or German) in the written and oral form

© KONINKLIJKE BRILL NV, LEIDEN, 2019 | DOI:10.1163/9789004394377_004

according to the guidelines by the Polish Ministry of Education. The students have a choice between a written exam in a basic form or advanced form. The majority of students select English for their final exam.

During the three years of high school, the English teachers are expected to follow a state-mandated curriculum that specifies what they are required to teach in terms of grammar and vocabulary. The language teachers are required to prepare students in order for them to possess linguistic knowledge in the following 13 areas:

1. *Human Being*: Clothes and fashion, body language: ways of looking, body language: ways of speaking, body language: posture and gesture, personality, feelings-idioms, attitudes and beliefs, and the mind.

2. *House and Home*: Types of houses and flats, outside the house, furniture and furnishings, adjectives to describe interiors, neighborhoods, real estate, maintenance and redecorations, phrasal verbs, house and home-idioms.

3. *School*: Types of schools, at university, the education system, school objects, school subjects and school work, learning, problems and solutions, assessments and examinations, idioms.

4. *Work*: Jobs, adjectives to describe jobs, departments in a company, people at work, work and money, employment and the job market, idioms.

5. *Family and Social Life*: Relatives, family celebrations-birth, family celebrations-weddings, family celebrations-funerals, other celebrations, family arrangements, family and money, friends and acquaintances, relationships, leisure time, phrasal verbs, idioms.

6. *Food, Groceries, Shopping and Services*: Food, nutrients, preparing food, idioms, types of shops, at the checkout, bargains, high prices, paying, complaining, banking.

7. *Traveling and Tourism*: Types of holidays, accommodation, journeys and trips, means of travel, rail travel, air travel, sea travel, road travel and driving, cycling, phrasal verbs, idioms.

8. *Culture*: Music, visual art, literature, film, theater, the media, adjectives to talk about art, audiences, idioms.

9. *Health and Sport*: The human body, sickness and health, phrasal verbs, diseases, injuries, disabilities, health care, professionals, idioms: saying how people are, sports, sports equipment, verb collocations.

10. *Science and Technology*: Areas of science, scientists, scientific research and discovery, technology, information and communication technology, using simple appliances, phrasal verbs, idioms.

11. *Nature*: Landscape, features, plants, animals, weather, natural disasters, the environments, idioms.

12. *Government and Society*: The structure of government, civil rights and liberties, socio-political issues, the economy, war and conflicts, crime, phrasal verbs, idioms.

13. *Elements of Knowledge about English in other English-Speaking Countries* (*besides the United Kingdom and the United States*): Ireland, Australia, Canada, and India (Umińska et al., 2014, p. 4).

The students have between three and six 45 minutes-long English classes per week. There are about 30 students in each class, but for the purpose of teaching and learning English, the class is divided by level into two groups with no more than 15–17 students in each group. The five research participants were given the following pseudonyms: participant one, Anna; participant two, Barbara; participant three, Helena; participant four, Lidia; and participant five, Maria. The reason I selected these pseudonyms is because I wanted my participants to sound like humans who have voices, otherwise the terms participant one, participant two, participant three, participant four, and participant five would give this research a robotic, non-human and technical dimension, which I tried to avoid. The pseudonyms were carefully selected, and the names are close equivalents of the names in English for the native English-speaking potential readers of this research, so it is easier for them to read the names. Table 4.1 is an overview of the high school EFL teaching participants.

TABLE 4.1.   The participating teachers

Participant number	Age	Education	Years of experience
One Anna	47 years old	Master's Degree in English as a Foreign Language	24 years of experience teaching English in a public high school
Two Barbara	44 years old	Master's Degree in English as a Foreign Language	22 years of experience teaching English in a public high school
Three Helena	43 years old	Master's Degree in English as a Foreign Language	20 years of experience teaching English in a public high school
Four Lidia	32 years old	Master's Degree in English as a Foreign Language	11 years of experience teaching English in a public high school
Five Maria	48 years old	Master's Degree in English as a Foreign Language	23 years of experience teaching English in a public high school

Development of Students' Speaking, Communicative, and Cooperative Skills through Interviews and Class Observations

The data described here is selective. It concentrates mainly on presenting the data associated with the development of speaking, communicative, and cooperative skills and omits the development of reading and writing skills, which were also present during the classroom observations, though, not relevant to the topic of this research.

Portrait of Each of the Participants

In the following sections I have broken my observations down to a focus on each of the participants. This data was created for each participant on the basis of face-to-face interviews and face-to-face classroom observations.

Portrait of Participant One: Anna

Interviews

Anna has a Master's Degree in teaching EFL. She represents the British English version of English in terms of speaking, pronunciation, vocabulary, and spelling. She has been teaching English for over 24 years. Anna herself started learning English in the seventh grade. She recalls that the lessons back then represented a traditional Grammatical/Grammar-Based Approach with drills, rote memorization, plenty of grammatical exercises, and almost no speaking English in class by students.

Anna enjoyed learning English, despite the fact that during communist government control, learning a language neither consider life outside of the classroom, nor the socio-cultural aspects of languages. However, Anna was very fortunate to have a family in Great Britain, and through visits there she was able to use and improve her knowledge of English while living in an authentic environment of the English language.

Anna truly fell in love with the English language in high school, when one day her teacher of English invited a native speaker of English from Great Britain to the class, and Anna observed her teacher speaking English fluently with the visitor. It was the spark that caused Anna to think to herself, "I want to do the same. I want to speak English so fluently as well."

Anna's teacher of English was a very charismatic woman, but the English language process itself was quite monotonous, because that is what the communist educational authority required. All the teachers were required to use the same textbooks, which were unappealing and had almost no illustrations. Each lesson in the textbook looked the same; there was a reading, new vocabulary was explained through a direct translation from English to Polish, and students were required to do a few exercises concerning the readings. The teacher of English attempted to make the English lessons more interesting by bringing in authentic newspaper readings and some texts in English issued by publishers in the Soviet Union. It was not easy, as there were about 34 students in the class and the classes were never divided into smaller groups.

Anna selected English for her final high school oral exam. She recalls that the exam was much easier than the oral exams her student currently experience, as at the time, access to methodological materials was much less than it is today. This is partly the result of modern technology. As Anna decided to study the English language at a university, she also had a private tutor to prepare her for the entrance exam because being accepted to study EFL at a university was very competitive in Poland in the 1980s.

During her university studies, Anna was most interested in teaching the English language and the methodology of teaching EFL. She recalls the methodology was quite revolutionary for her and eye-opening for the end of the 1980s in communist Poland. She learned how to present various grammatical aspects and vocabulary in an interesting way and saw the value of games, warm-ups, and hands-on activities.

Anna claims the methodology classes contributed to the kind of a teacher she is presently. She remembers three important steps in the EFL methodology: introduction of a grammatical or lexical issue, practicing, consolidation, and revision. Anna admits at the university she did not learn about the importance of speaking, communication, and cooperation in learning English, or of using dialogs, drama, theater, and cultural aspects when teaching a foreign language. She also did not learn at that time about the importance of authentic learning, a connection between students' identity and learning English, and the association between the outside world and learning English. These are important ideas in teaching EFL that Anna learned about after graduation through workshops, trainings, and conferences she attended while she was already a high school EFL teacher. However, Anna only realized the importance of contact with the native English language through her exposure to native English speaking teachers. It is her education, personal development through training, workshops and conferences, and her teaching experience, which are the factors that contribute to what kind of teacher she is today.

In response to the question concerning how Anna teaches now and how she focuses on the development of her students' speaking, communicative, and cooperative skills, she stated, "I try to connect teaching with reality." She provided some examples. For instance, after a strong wind Anna saw a broken tree outside of the classroom. She asked her students to express their ideas about this object. Another time when she checked the attendance list, she asked her students why they were present at the lesson and the selected students were then expected to present 30-second speeches on the topic.

Anna shows her students various movies and videos on YouTube, where students have opportunities to discuss what they saw, usually in pairs first, and then share their observations with the whole class. Their observations generally include the content of the visual materials, new vocabulary, and grammatical structures. For instance, she and her students watched some parts of *Sherlock Holmes* (Richie, 2009) and then shared what they had seen as a way to practice their English-speaking skills.

Anna also uses songs, not only for different holidays, such as Christmas carols, but also songs that are popular and liked by students at a given time. Anna realizes that it is important to connect students' interests with their learning, and when the connection takes place, students learn much more willingly with far more enthusiasm. Usually with songs, the students learn new vocabulary through exercises such as scrambling the lines of song lyrics, which then the students are asked to put the lyrics in order or to fill in the blanks of the lyrics while listening to a given song.

While doing reading exercises Anna is not satisfied with a multiple choice answer but asks her students to justify their answers and show in a text a proof for their justification. This results in deeper learning as students gain confidence in choosing their selections. She also selects important sayings or proverbs from texts and asks the students to make speeches about them, in which students are also entitled to their own opinions and can transform the speeches into group and class discussions.

Anna also uses games such as *Hangman*, usually for the purpose of reviewing new vocabulary. She uses other games for the same purpose as well. For instance, she provides her students with a word and selects a student who needs to come up with a recently learned word starting with the last letter of the previous word. Anna also organizes class debates when students express their opinions supporting or opposing the thesis. For example, "Are you for or against the death penalty?"

Anna uses numerous materials from previous final exams in English, not only to prepare her students for the exams, but also because the majority of the exemplary exams are of high quality which contributes to the development of students' speaking, communicative, and cooperative skills. She asks her students to create scenarios for role-play activities with a specific focus on the new vocabulary and grammatical structures they recently learned. The role-plays give students opportunities to work in small groups and, in this way develop, their speaking, communicative, cooperative, and negotiating skills, which are so useful in the world outside the classroom. Then the role-plays are presented, recorded, and analyzed in an oral form by the students in terms of content and form. Sometimes Anna asks her students to prepare dialogs in pairs with the same follow-up procedure as in group activities.

Anna also utilizes materials from First Certificate in English (FCE) exams, which is an upper-intermediate, international English language qualification used at colleges, universities, and higher education institutions as proof of everyday written and spoken English for work and study purposes (University of English ESOL Examinations, 2011). She also utilizes materials from the Cambridge Proficiency Exam (CPE), which tests English ability at the highest possible level and demonstrates that a candidate can communicate with fluency approaching that of a native English speaker. Many businesses and educational institutions accept the CPE worldwide as proof that a candidate has mastered English at an exceptional level (Cambridge English Proficiency, 2015). These are also the exams used for foreign students who wish to enter colleges and universities in the United Kingdom. They are equivalent to the Test of English as a Foreign Language (TOEFL) exam, which is a standardized test of English language proficiency for non-native English language speakers wishing to enroll in U.S. and Canadian colleges and universities (TOEFL, 2005/2006).

Anna reflected on the change in her ways of teaching, she said that her teaching changed over the last 20 years, not only because communism fell in Poland in 1989 and the situation enabled Polish EFL teachers more contact with Western teaching methodologies, especially coming from Great Britain and the United States, but also because the methodologies changed overall in English speaking countries. They became more student-centered and stressed the importance of developing students' speaking, communicative, and cooperative skills.

Teaching has always been a passion for Anna. Therefore, with time she was able to change textbooks from traditional to more student-friendly ones, with colorful materials, having a lot of images, audio tapes, and later CDs included. She introduced cultural and geographical elements to her teaching, e.g., sports in the United Kingdom, the Grand Canyon, Thanksgiving and such. Some of the new generation textbooks came with cultural and geographical materials, and some Anna recorded from the BBC and the Discovery Channel. She uses authentic materials, such as from Mary Glasgow publications and Newsweek Magazine. She uses the Internet and images on a daily basis to increase her students' knowledge of the English language, and to create a more authentic and visual experience for her students. With more and more time, gaining more experience, practice, and expertise, Anna now organizes open lessons where other EFL teachers are able to observe and learn from her way of conducting English lessons.

In order to make her students' English language experience even more authentic, every year, Anna organizes English language camps to England, Wales, Ireland, or Scotland. Before the trips, she presents some realia to her students, so that students can see, touch, and even smell a kilt, a bagpipe, and other realia. During communist times, similar trips as such were impossible for teachers and students desiring to visit Britain for linguistic and cultural purposes because of economic and political reasons (Reichelt, 2005).

Anna always tries to make a connection between her students' learning and their reality and the usefulness of the English language after students graduate. She shared an anecdote with me. Some years ago she was teaching her students new vocabulary, and among various words and phrases there was "a fork-lift truck." One student mentioned with skepticism, "Why do we learn words like this? We will never use this type of vocabulary in real life." A few years passed, the student graduated, and later visited Anna and said that he had a job now in Britain where he worked on a fork-lift truck. Anna and the student had a good laugh about the linguistic situation, and Anna tells the story to her students when they doubt the usefulness of learning some more sophisticated, formal, and academic (Cognitive Academic Language Proficiency (CALP) type of vocabulary and language (Cummins, 1991).

Anna does not remember particular methods she learned during her university studies, but she believes that using one method would not be appropriate to students anyways, as it would lead to students' boredom, routine, and monotony in the classroom. She believes in diversity in terms of activities she uses with her students. English lessons should involve plenty of opportunities for students to speak, and interact, connect with students' interests and reality surrounding them, and involve authentic materials, realia, images, and technology.

Classroom Observations

From the middle of February to the middle of May 2015, I observed Anna in her classroom. Anna has her own EFL classroom where she teaches, and her students from all the groups she teaches come to this classroom for their English lessons. The classroom is sunny with big windows, and painted yellow. The walls are decorated with posters of kings and queens of Great Britain. It has a whiteboard, however, it is not equipped with an interactive board. The EFL room is at the same time a computer room, thus it was equipped with 17 computers for the students to work individually.

In order to promote speaking skills in her students, Anna spoke about 95 percent in English to her students, and they in turn were also expected to respond in English as well. The classes she taught were the most advanced of all groups observed, and they were scheduled to take the final exam in English in May of 2015. The Polish language was used only if absolutely necessary to understand the most crucial parts of a given lesson. For example, to avoid ambiguity in understanding some grammatical nuisances, particular items of vocabulary, and so forth. Anna focused on developing her students' speaking skills especially when it came to the topics within a general theme required (one of the above 13 themes) to be overviewed for the final exam.

On one occasion, the topic was friendship. Previously, students were supposed to find a quote in English on the topic of friendship and to share it with the whole class. Anna then connected the quotes with a real life situation and asked the students about friendships in their personal lives. When moments of silence occurred, she prompted students and initiated the class into a whole class discussion, asking questions such as, "Is friendship more important than family, why/why not"? "Is friendship for lifetime, why/why not?" Should employees in a company become friends, why/why not"? Anna made sure that each student contributed to the discussion, thus all the students had the opportunity to practice their speaking skills in English. Through this activity the students had an occasion to share their personal thoughts and ideas. They were able to identify the topic of the lesson and connect it to their lives outside of the classroom, reflect on friendships in their personal lives, and obviously they were practicing their speaking skills.

On another occasion, Anna was observed teaching her students vocabulary on the topic of family and family celebrations. She never underestimated her students' prior knowledge and asked if they knew a given word or phrase. With unknown vocabulary, for example, she provided a picture of a family tree, and by pointing to appropriate characters, she said, "This is your niece and this is your nephew." In some cases, Anna provided descriptive definitions of words and phrases. For example, "a mother-in law" is the mother of your husband or wife when you get married. Then she connected the topic of family members to students' personal lives by providing them an opportunity to share information about their families. When moments of silence occurred, she prompted her students to continue discussing family by asking questions such as, "Would you like to be married and have children, why/why not"? "Is the age 18 too young to be married and start a family, why/why not"? Students had multiple opportunities to practice their speaking skills.

During the next class, Anna talked with students about family celebrations. When talking about weddings, she used a whiteboard and drew a chart of "wedding" with connecting words such as: groom, bride, best man, etc. Then to connect with real life outside of the classroom, she asked her students if they had seen the movie *Four Weddings and a Funeral* (Newell, 1994). Then there was a discussion about the movie. Some female students also shared information about a show they had watched concerning wedding dresses. Anna easily redirected a misbehaving student's attention by asking him what kind of wedding he would like to have. This activity enabled students to broaden their vocabulary on the topic of family and family celebration through visuals (family tree, wedding chart on the whiteboard) and word definitions in English. Students were also able to practice their speaking skills and identify themselves within the class topic.

At the end of the discussion on the topic of family and family celebrations, a student prepared a PowerPoint presentation on wedding traditions in different countries such as Scotland, England, Morocco, Egypt, Japan, and Pakistan. Anna conducted the presentation fully in English and provided multiple pictures, enriching the topic of wedding traditions. The activity took the students beyond the four walls of the classroom and provided them a multicultural opportunity to practice their speaking skills by asking the presenter questions on the various wedding celebrations in different countries.

While talking about another family celebration, birth for example, Anna introduced new vocabulary in English such as diaper and pacifier. Again, she connected the topic with real life situations as the class talked about newborn babies in their own families. Anna asked *Wh* questions, such as "Is it easy or difficult to raise children, why/why not"? "Is raising a family for everyone, why/why not"?

The last family celebration that students had an opportunity to talk about was funeral, again learning new vocabulary associated with the topic. Even though the topic is sad, it is very realistic, connected with real life and identifiable with students' lives. On the topic of funerals, Anna asked the students if they saw the TV series *Six Feet Under* (Ball, 2001–2005), and the students who had shared their ideas on the show. Next, Anna put her students into pairs and they were asked to talk about funerals in their families by practicing this new vocabulary. The talks were connected with the reality of Poland and the Catholic tradition of funerals, as the majority of the students are Catholic. During the discussion on funerals, the students had an opportunity to identify with their reality, regardless of its sad nature, by connecting with the religious traditions of the students' native country. This allowed them to practice their speaking skills, and working in pairs they were able to practice their communicative and cooperative skills with partners.

During another class, students were divided into pairs, and they were supposed to prepare a dialog about travelling to Tasmania, using vocabulary from the last three classes concerning the broader theme of travelling. Then the students performed the dialog in front of the whole class. The students were strongly encouraged to create the authentic atmosphere of a trip to Tasmania by modulating their voices and using such emotional expressions like "it is splendid," "it was gorgeous, I have never experienced anything like that before in my life," and so forth.

The students were also strongly encouraged to speak and improvise when necessary and encouraged not to read scripts word for word when acting out their dialogs. Other students were to write down the new vocabulary they heard in the dialogs, e.g., wilderness. The pair work configuration activity provided students with an opportunity to practice their communicative and cooperative skills to prepare a successfully-sounding authentic dialog and to practice their speaking skills. Through the dialogs the students were able to review the new vocabulary and consolidated it in their learning.

On one occasion, Anna was observed to discuss spontaneously a topic that was not a part of a lesson. A student walked into the classroom and shared happy news that he passed his driver's license test. Anna congratulated him and developed the situation into a topic for discussion in English. Students shared their thoughts on driving and their struggles associated with passing the test. Anna then engaged her students in a discussion about whether they should be allowed to take the driver's exam at the age of 17, why/why not? and if young people should be allowed to drink alcohol at the age of 18, why/why not?

I was also able to share my knowledge about the rules to obtain a driver's license in the United States and my own experience associated with obtaining my own driver's license. Through this discussion, the students who were aged 17 and 18 were able not only to practice their speaking skills in English but share their ideas concerning the Polish reality of obtaining a driver's license, a matter that greatly concerned them, and learn about the regulations of obtaining a driver's license in the United States.

Anna devoted one lesson to the notion of idioms. She introduced them in connection with the importance of knowing academic, advanced, and more sophisticated vocabulary. On this occasion, paired students were working together in the computer lab. The students were asked to talk about idioms and search for definitions of each idiom online. Then the students shared their definitions with the whole class.

Next, Anna asked her students if they thought idioms were important when using English. Those who were for using idioms sat on one side of the classroom and those who were against sat on the opposite side of the class. Each group had to prepare a list of arguments supporting their statements. Anna monitored the debate that followed, valuing each student's opinion as long as they presented coherent, logical, and convincing arguments. Anna then introduced her students to a chain activity: each student had to present one favorite idiom she/he learned in a previous class and explain why she/he liked it the most. The next student then had to say her/his idiom and the previous person's idiom. The activity continued until all the students presented their idioms. During this lesson, the students were able to practice their speaking, cooperative (chain activity), and communicative skills (pair work) while debating their arguments using technology in their process of learning. The students also practiced their memory skills, as they learned new idioms through repetition. They paid attention and felt motivated because Anna randomly selected a student to present her/his idioms and repeat the previous idioms presented by their classmates.

For almost every class, Anna prepared a short visual activity for her students as a practice for their oral final exam. For example, she presented a picture of a family gathering, and the students were expected to answer questions starting with "Where/who/what is/are/she/he/they doing in a given picture?" The students were also able to relate to the picture and talked about gatherings in their own families. During the activity, the students were able to practice their speaking skills and identify with the topic and their own family.

During another class, students were asked to find a picture of an ancient or modern painting, or sculpture and research about the author and the art. They then shared ideas and opinions about it and explained why they selected that particular piece. Some students brought hard copies of pictures; some used technology and presented their images on laptops, tablets and/or cell phones. Through the activity, the students were able to practice their speaking skills and broaden their general content area knowledge on the topic of art, while learning from each other.

Another time in order to practice for the oral final exam, Anna asked her students to imagine they were in England and wanted to sign up for a sports class. The students working with their elbow partners were asked to communicate and address four areas: What sport is it going to be and why? How will you pay for it? Where will it be? How will you get there? Even though the students prepared the exercise with their elbow partners, the teacher selected two random students, and they had to improvise the dialog to practice for the final oral exam, as during the exam students will have to improvise with an examiner. During this activity, the students were able to practice their speaking, communicative, cooperative, and improvisational skills.

When making her students practice their speaking, communicative, and cooperative skills, Anna also kept in mind teaching her students real life skills. In

Poland, often job applicants are interviewed for employment in English. There-fore, Anna asked the students to prepare a job interview between an employer and a potential employee. The students were able to use electronic devices to search for vocabulary associated with the topic of job interviews. Then she played a video in English concerning the appropriate dress code for a job interview.

During the last observed class, the students were asked to act out the job interviews. Several pairs presented their work in front of the whole class. They simulated the job interview, they were properly dressed, and arranged a table and chairs as if it was a real office. Through this activity, the students were able to practice their speaking, communicative, cooperative, and improvisational skills and engaged the skills necessary for the real world job market outside of the four-wall classroom setting.

In the observed classes, Anna demonstrated the importance of student-centered teaching (the connection of teaching with student's reality and inter-ests), using authentic materials, technology, and interaction through Total Groups, Pairs, Small Groups and Individual work group configurations, defined in short as TPSI (Herrera & Murry, 2011). This was not a change overnight. It felt as if it was a gradual and natural change through the years.

Textbooks Anna uses for teaching EFL are:

– Evans, V., & Edwards, L. (2008). *Upstream advanced*. Newbury Berkshire, UK: Express.
– Umińska, M., Hastings, B., Chandler, D., Fricker, R., & Trapnell, B. (2014). *English: Repetytorium maturalne*. Warszawa, Poland: Longman/Pearson.

Portrait of Participant Two: Barbara

Interviews

Barbara has a Master's Degree in teaching EFL and represents the British Eng-lish version in terms of speaking, pronunciation, vocabulary, and spelling. She has been teaching English for over 22 years. Barbara always wanted to be a teacher, even though the teaching profession does not run in her family. Dur-ing family gatherings she improvised being a teacher, and her cousins were her students. During middle school she always liked foreign languages, and because the Russian language was compulsory at that time, Barbara decided to become a teacher of Russian, even though the classes were taught in a tra-ditional grammar translation way, with a lot of vocabulary to memorize and grammar structure to practice without context.

Barbara's mother also enrolled her in additional English classes, and she fell in love with the English language, even though the classes were traditional like the Russian classes, they had a component that really interested her. She remembers her teacher of English was quite revolutionary for the early 1980s in Poland, and despite the fact the textbooks were very traditional, grammar-oriented, and based on repetitions, drills, and memorization, the teacher brought in lots of realia, and the students learned a lot of English vocabulary in this way. "The students were allowed to touch and smell the realia. It was fantastic," she said. Barbara attended private English lessons as well at that time, and she knew that her future would be connected with the language.

When Barbara entered high school she already had some foundations of English. In high school she had seven hours of English per week. She considers herself fortunate to have had an English teacher for four years who was revolutionary for her times and that made the lessons very appealing. Unfortunately, the textbooks were very traditional, unappealing, and saturated with grammar and generic dialogs but Barbara's teacher was able to turn it into an adventure. The teacher was experimenting in the class. She introduced creativity into her teaching and she used to surprise the students. She introduced role-play, drama, had the students create scenarios, threw out topics that provoked them to think, brainstorm, express their ideas, and use their emotions while using English. Despite the fact that it was communist times, where there was no technology and access to authentic literature in English was limited, the teacher brought some articles in English. Sometimes they were Russian editions in English, and the students were able to choose the articles according to their interests and liking. According to Barbara, her teacher did an extraordinary job of teaching English.

After Barbara graduated from high school, she was accepted to the Teachers' College of English. During her education, she had very traditional, lecture-oriented professors who were very well informed theoreticians. In this college there were also professors who had a progressive approach towards teaching methodologies, who treated students as partners in the process of teaching and learning. They motivated them to speak, to communicate and work in pairs and groups, and to create projects.

After Barbara had finished college, she attended and graduated from a Master's English program and became a teacher. At the beginning she worked in a language school from 1991–1993. She used very traditional textbooks, as it was required in the school. She used a lot of drills, repetitions, grammar teaching, and grammar translation, because "A language teacher's job has been understood differently at different times and in different settings. Traditionally, the function of the teacher was to transmit knowledge, give instructions and control the process of student language learning" (Wierbińska, 2009).

However, Barbara tried to use a lot of English when communicating with her students.

In 1993, Barbara started working in a public high school when for the first time she was able to introduce a progressive book for the times. It was the *Headway* British textbook series. The textbook focused on the development of all four literacy skills: listening, speaking, reading, and writing. There was less pressure on grammar, and it was taught in a cultural context. The textbook was printed on glossy paper with plenty of attractive pictures.

Answering the question of how her teaching had changed, she said that it did change because at the beginning of her teaching career she was imitating her high school teacher's ways of teaching, which as mentioned previously used theater, role-play, and drama. Barbara also used these type of activities in her classes. She included additional articles in English, focusing in particular on the cultural, historical, and geographical aspects of the United Kingdom because it was easier to obtain British materials than American. However, recently the tools for teaching have changed, as there was more access to information coming from the larger English-speaking world and authentic materials through the Internet.

Currently, Barbara uses materials from the BBC, YouTube, and other digital resources. Contemporary textbooks are now equipped with multimedia tools. There is also more information in the textbooks concerning culture, geography, history, and political science of Great Britain and the United States. As a result of her reflections, Barbara sees that before she was teaching English per se, within the four walls of the classroom. Now she teaches a lot of information with the help of a tool called "the English language." Today, the textbooks are of high quality in terms of content, but what changed is the pressure to teach to vocabulary and grammar to the final exam. The rules about how best to teach English also change frequently, which requires patience and flexibility. Barbara feels that "It is important that if materials are not too interesting when it comes to content, they have to be interesting when it comes to the form." To know students by their names and what they are interested in so you can adjust the materials and techniques of working with them is important. In this way the students see that they are valued and their opinions are appreciated, which creates a positive atmosphere in the classroom.

Barbara uses plenty of images, visuals, and pair and group projects. For example, once when she was teaching about the judicial system, she asked the students to participate in a play where the setting was in a courtroom, and then they held a debate where students had to argue if they were for or against the death penalty. Using this method, students were able to use their opinions and express their emotions and feelings. It was a motivating way of learning new vocabulary about the judicial system. Barbara's motto is "Tell me and I forget, teach me and I may remember, involve me and I learn." This quote is originally a Chinese proverb also attributed to Benjamin Franklin (Schultz, 2013).

According to Barbara, there are two sources of motivation for the students to learn English. One is that that they have to pass a foreign language exam to graduate from high school and the majority chooses English. Two is that the students communicate via the Internet with people from all over the world. The students are able to travel either with parents or go on organized school trips to experience English as the medium of communication regardless of the country they visit. Times have changed and English is not only taught within the four walls of the classroom anymore. Barbara organizes language camps in Great Britain to enable the students to have contact with an authentic environment of English.

Barbara tries to motivate her students to make them want to actively participate during lessons. She has been learning new activities from conferences, workshops, and projects for EFL teachers. Many textbook publishing companies also organize various meetings as well. She wants her classes to be interactive with the use of technology. She uses a lot of the examination materials from previous years and from FCE and CPE (sources explained and described under Anna). She believes that students should be active agents in the process of their education.

When it comes to developing the four skills of listening, speaking, reading, and writing, Barbara tries to incorporate all of them, but it is not always possible in the same lesson. As far as listening is concerned, she includes many recorded materials. She uses BBC videos, news videos, and short clips and then motivates her students to talk about them. She likes videos because they reinforce teaching English with visual materials, which is more interesting to students and teachers of English than just audio materials. Barbara incorporates them according to a given topic from the required 13 subject areas, listed above. She also uses YouTube and video-based materials that come with the textbooks. She thinks that the textbooks they have now in schools are of high quality. Often the listening exercises are multiple-choice exercises. However, Barbara always has her students explain why he/she selected a given answer. Sometimes, in accordance with her students' interests, as she believes in autonomous education, Barbara brings texts of song lyrics and while listening, the students are required to fill in the blanks of words or phrases.

Christmas carols are a must before Christmas. After the song activities, Barbara sings together with her students. She also brings movies to watch but it is never watching for the pleasure of watching. The activity is always accompanied by questions and exercises the students need to do during or after the movie and to check for understanding and have students broaden their English vocabulary. One of students' favorite movies is *A Christmas Carol* (Zemeckis, 2009).

The development of speaking skills, according to Barbara, must be built on the foundation of possessing a certain amount of vocabulary and grammatical structures on a given topic, especially with the younger students. The more advanced they are in English, the more they are able to talk spontaneously on any topic: express their opinions, emotions, facts, and agree or disagree. Barbara asks her students to prepare speeches on a given topic. However, to have all the students active while one student presents a speech, the rest of the students sit with their chairs in a horseshoe shape and prepare questions for the presenter.

Barbara uses various TPSI group configurations. She says the variation is crucial to avoid boredom but also to make sure that students communicate and cooperate with one another. Besides, it also provides opportunities for students to be in configurations that everyone likes. Some students, including those that are extroverts, prefer pair and small group work, while other students, who often are introverts, prefer to be in a total group or work individually. The various TPSI group configurations help to build integration and interaction in a given class.

Barbara said, "Visualization is very important in the process of teaching and learning a language." She provided an example of how she visually teaches her students the Present Perfect Continuous Tense, a tense frequently difficult for beginners to comprehend, as it is a tense that does not exist in the Polish language. The example is as follows: "Imagine a little girl with a piece of chocolate. Her face is smudged with the chocolate. Do you see her? Do you see her dirty face? Do you see the chocolate wrap in the garbage (making the move of throwing the chocolate wrap in the garbage can)? I tell her *"Have you been eating chocolate?"* Whenever doing grammatical exercises with students when there is the Present Perfect Continuous Tense present, Barbara says, "That is the girl eating chocolate tense, do you remember?" The students answer, "Oh yes, we remember," and they smile.

In terms of teaching methods, Barbara does not recall particular theoretical methods or models, but she does not find that important, because she would not use one method anyway, as it would be too much of a routine and monotony for the students. Through her years and experience, she has been improving her ways of teaching and achieving the goal to create conditions that would optimally increase her students' English language skills. As Barbara mentioned before, she imitated her own teachers and professors at first, and over the years she has been changing and adding new teaching strategies and activities to contribute to her students' success in their process of learning English.

Classroom Observations

From the middle of February to the middle of May 2015, I observed Barbara in her classroom. Barbara has her own permanent EFL classroom, while her students came to her. The classroom is sunny, painted yellow, and with big windows. The walls are decorated with a map of the United Kingdom of Great Britain and Northern Ireland and posters of popular travelling places in London. The EFL room is equipped with a whiteboard and a closet where Barbara keeps her teaching materials, such as textbooks, dictionaries, and a CD player. The EFL room is not equipped with computers but it is equipped with an interactive board compatible with textbook materials where students can do exercises moving various part and words with their fingers on the interactive board.

Barbara uses English almost all the time in her classes, and students are strongly encouraged to respond in English as well. She uses the British pronunciation, grammar and vocabulary. The native language is used only if absolutely necessary to explain and understand the English vocabulary required in an assignment.

When explaining grammar, Barbara wants to make sure the students understand the rules and use of grammatical components. When teaching grammar, Barbara makes sure students practice the grammatical components in the oral form in connection with real life situations. For example, when she teaches modal verbs, such as "must" and "must not," she provides prompts, such as "young people must give up seats designated for disabled and elderly people," or "you must not smoke in school," then she asks students to respond to the phrases. In this way, the students not only have an opportunity to speak English but express their ideas as well.

When practicing modal verbs Barbara used pair work configurations. Students practiced dialogs with elbow partners, and then she selected two different students who were not sitting next to each other, to create a dialog using modal verbs that were practiced in the class. The students not only had an opportunity to practice modal verbs in the spoken form and be creative, they also practiced their communicative and cooperative skills.

Barbara used visuals in teaching modal verbs. She brought in authentic magazine pictures and students were asked to describe the pictures using modal verbs. For example, one picture showed two young people who looked angry. A student said, "They must be arguing." Another picture presented three people running and getting to the finish line. A student using a modal verb remarked,

"They must be tired." Students were encouraged to use their imagination and talk more about the pictures. This picture activity gave students an opportunity to practice modal verbs, speculate what was going on in the pictures, and speak/practice their English.

Barbara, whenever possible, attempted to connect lesson topics to students' reality. For instance, she connected the theme of a picture of people running in a marathon and a student's real situation by asking, "Wiktoria, your mom is a marathon runner, could you share some more information about it?" And the student did. Then, Barbara asked some more questions about running, marathons, and the Olympic Games involved students in a discussion in English. In this way, students were practicing their English skills, and they were able to express their thoughts and opinions, have the feeling that their opinions mattered, and took the lesson beyond the confinement of the four classroom walls.

When explaining new vocabulary, Barbara never underestimated students' previous knowledge. She asked her students for the meaning of particular words and for them to offer definitions in English, providing an opportunity for the students to speak English.

On one occasion, Barbara taught personality adjectives. She presented such adjectives as affectionate, conscientious, sensible, and modest. She asked her students to work with their elbow partners using English-English dictionaries (English-Polish and Polish-English dictionaries were not allowed) to find definitions of the adjectives. One dictionary per pair was provided. As the students continued to work with their elbow partners, they were asked to describe the partners using a new adjective, and justify why a given student possessed that given personality adjective. This exercise provided students with an opportunity to practice their speaking, communicative, and cooperative skills, and to use new vocabulary when working with their elbow partners. The activity was also connected with their reality. It is an example of a natural way of learning English, as students were talking about themselves.

In order to practice students' speaking skills, Barbara used various themes for discussions in accordance with the final exam requirements. One of the topics I observed in use was the theme of travelling. Barbara provided her students with a situation where they were in England, and they were traveling with a friend. They had to address the length of the trip, means of transportation, boarding, and things that needed to be taken with them. Working in pairs, students discussed the requirements and wrote dialogs in the form of scripts, which they later acted out. The required task provided students with an opportunity to practice their speaking, communicative, and cooperative skills. Barbara stressed the importance of speaking instead of reading the dialogs, to give students a more authentic sense of the use of English.

As homework, students were asked to work individually and to select an image that could be connected with the learned personality adjectives. During the next class, students presented their pictures and talked about them. It was an activity that required the students to practice their speaking skills.

In order to practice students' debating skills, Barbara showed two pictures to her students: one of a student, studying in a classroom, and the other a student studying at home. The class was divided into two groups. One group was asked to prepare arguments supporting class schooling and the other group was supposed to prepare arguments supporting homeschooling. The groups first prepared arguments on posters. Then the debate started, monitored by Barbara. The activity provided an opportunity for the students to practice their logical thinking, argumentative, speaking, communicative, and cooperative skills.

One day Barbara read a story, *A Poor Traveler*. She stimulated her students' imagination by asking questions such as: "What does it mean to be poor as a traveler"? "Is it about money"? "Is it about poor traveling plans?" To answer these questions, Barbara had her students brainstorm, speculate, and use their imagination when practicing their speaking skills. Barbara read the story to the students, except the ending. The students again speculated what the ending of the story might be. They had another opportunity to practice their speaking skills.

Then in groups of three, Barbara had the students act the story out. They could choose whom they wanted to work with. They prepared some decorations, divided their roles, and improvised the story. They were very enthusiastic about the project. The students were able to organize themselves into groups, which gave them a feeling of ownership of their own learning. Through the activity, students were able to be creative and practice their speaking, communicative, and cooperative skills. Through the group project, students were also able to practice skills such as flexibility, patience, and tolerance, skills so necessary in their future lives and to be able to work as a team in the professional world.

Barbara is a student-centered educator who provides multiple opportunities for her students to be creative, imaginative and to develop their speaking, communicative, cooperative and debating, argumentative, and logical thinking skills. She creates an authentic environment where students can connect the class material with real life situations and their interests, and where they feel free and safe to express their thoughts and ideas.

Textbooks Barbara uses for teaching EFL are:
- Evans, V. (2015). *Use of English*. Kraków, Poland: Egis.
- McKinley, S. Hastings, B., & Raczyńska, R. (2012). *New matura success*. Warszawa, Poland: Longman/Pearson.

Portrait of Participant Three: Helena

Interviews

Helena has a Master's Degree in teaching EFL and represents the British English version in terms of speaking, pronunciation, vocabulary, and spelling. She has been teaching English for over 20 years. Helena's adventure with English started with her parents. Her mother, who was a special education teacher, had to find creative ways to reach her students and advised Helena to become a teacher. Her father, who knows German and English fluently, also supported Helena in becoming a teacher. He got her interested in the English language, as he recognized language skills in his daughter. Helena learned English in neither elementary, nor middle school. She chose to be in an English language-focused high school class, where she had six hours of English per week. It was stressful for Helena at the beginning of high school because there were students in her class who already knew some English, and it created a sense of competition. She was in the group in which no one had studied English before.

Helena was very ambitious to gain fluency in English as soon as possible. She bought several books, did exercises, and read articles to learn a lot of English on her own. She had family in Germany and during visits there, she was able to purchase English literature there, which was unavailable at that time in Poland. In Poland, she used Russian literature translated into the English language. In high school, Helena did not feel fortunate, as during her four years of high school she had four teachers of English and still had to learn a lot on her own. She did not experience much methodology during school and felt she was learning theoretical English on her own, with little practice. Therefore, it was very challenging for Helena, as she almost learned English by herself, but passed the final high school exam in English with high grades.

Helena's teachers of English in high school were very traditional. There was very little listening comprehension included in the materials and few audiotapes. Authentic English materials were especially limited. The teachers used a reel-to-reel audio tape recorder. The recordings they played were very generic and passive, nothing creative. The teachers played some generic dialogs or the students read them from textbooks. This was during communist times, so learning English was limited, and there was no access to Western methodologies. Helena described the methodology as "...passive, grammar translation methodology with a lot of grammar and sentence translation from English to Polish or Polish to English, and sentence transformation, where students had to change basic forms to grammatically appropriate forms in a given sentence." The teachers spoke Polish for most of the time in class. It was "dry teaching," as Helena called it.

Helena remembers one teacher in her senior year who was excellent. She had a new approach towards teaching and learning English. She spoke a lot of English in the classroom. She introduced some hands-on activities, like drawing road signs in English and describing them. The teacher used other visuals. She played videos and parts of movies, like *Dead Poets' Society* (Weir, 1989) in English. The teacher tried to connect learning English with the world outside of the four-walls classroom.

Next, Helena was accepted to the Teachers' College of English in Poland. She had Polish and American teachers there. The Polish professors were very traditional, formal, serious, conservative, and meticulous, and they kept their distance from students. However, they were very well informed and well-read with tremendous knowledge.

The American teachers were very different. They taught in a communicative way. Many of them were volunteers, thus did not always have methodological and pedagogical preparation, but they were open and accepting. They were focused on students speaking English and practicing the skill. Helena remembers having one American teacher who was a journalist by profession in a local newspaper somewhere in the United States. The discussions with him were very open. Once, for example, Helena and her classmates discussed birth control, which was a very progressive topic in a very Catholic Poland at the beginning of the 1990s. The American teachers used to bring interesting authentic materials to analyze the vocabulary. The topics of the articles were about life, and the discussions reached the reality outside of the classroom.

After Helena graduated from high school, she had reading and writing knowledge of English but she struggled with speaking the language. She was afraid of it because it was stressful when Polish teachers corrected her mistakes. Later on, she got cable TV and was able to listen and watch programs in English to enhance her knowledge of the English language. Her college years were the times when Helena opened herself and lost her fear of speaking English. As she communicated with the American teachers, her English-speaking skills improved. In terms of methodology, Helena's American teachers used a lot of group and paired-work activities. During discussions, the students were sitting on chairs set in a horseshoe shape. The classes were interactive and student-centered. No student was shy to share his/her observations.

Helena's past experienced with teaching as a student was very creative where student's opinion mattered. The atmosphere was very friendly. The experience made her become an innovative teacher. These activities helped Helena to be a better teacher herself, as she often incorporates these activities into her own teaching. She has been using new methods and enhancing them ever since. During her college years, Helena also learned word games, plays, drawing, and other active techniques. She learned from her first projects, remembering one in particular when she was searching to learn about American influences on post-communist Poland. Her topic was American technology in Poland, and she learned about all kinds of devices, such as saws, machines, and tractors.

Nowadays, Helena makes mini-projects with her students about British and American influences on the English language. Helena likes the concept of connecting the learning of English with the world. The methodology she learned from her American teachers in college had a big impact on what type of teacher she is today. The theory of teaching English presented by her Polish teachers is something Helena could have learned by herself from textbooks.

Helena graduated from college in 1995 and started working in a public high school as soon as she graduated from college. It was hard because she was given 26 contact hours to teach. She signed a contract to teach for another year. She was accepted into a Master's program in American literature. The program was very traditional, with lectures and discussions. She learned no teaching methodology in graduate school, finishing the program in 1998.

In her teaching career, Helena uses the communicative and cooperative approach with her students, but not as much as she would like to, because teaching to the final exams is time consuming and more important in Poland than developing students' communicative and cooperative skills. The exam creates pressure for the teachers and the students. Teaching grammar is not as important as it used to be but is still considered very important because it is a big part of the final exams in English.

However, Helena admits her students have more opportunities to speak and interact in her classes than when she was a student. Although there is so much pressure on teaching vocabulary, it is sophisticated vocabulary that students will probably never use in their lives. Helena compared the exams and competition questions of English from 1994 to today, and the ones from 1994 seemed so simple for the students. She does not even use books from the past, because they are too easy for the contemporary generation of students. There is such an availability of the materials in English through technology and Internet. Students also listen to music in English, watch movies in English, have friends all over the world. They chat, they text, they email, and the means of communication is obviously in English regardless of what country students and friends are from.

Students watch and read materials online and broaden their vocabulary. The teacher of English is not the only person passing the knowledge of English on to her/his students, but the students also learn English in private after-school English programs. Technology has changed the way Helena and other teachers of English teach. The students also see the practical usefulness of the English language in the world outside of school, and it makes sense to them to learn it.

Answering the question if it is easier or more difficult to teach English these days, Helena responded, "...it is easier and more difficult at the same time. Easier, because I have practice and experience and I know what works and what does not." She remembers what activities and ideas to use with which topics, vocabulary, and grammar structures. Teaching is more spontaneous and there is a wealth of hard copy materials, and Internet accessible materials to use. However, it is more difficult to teach English these days because it is not teaching English, but teaching to final exams. Helena said that there was an abundance of material to cover with the students, often at the cost that they speak, communicate, and cooperate less. Obviously, the exams are not only about grammar anymore as it used to be, because besides grammar, students also have to write an essay, converse with an examiner in English, and describe a picture. Still, the pressure of the exam is high, and the students have to know specific grammar and specific, sometimes rare vocabulary. The situation is not ideal, but Helena thinks it is positive that at least this change took place. Helena and other English teachers are aware of the importance of developing speaking, communicative, and cooperative skills in their students though.

Answering a question concerning the ways she develops speaking skills, Helena answered that as far as speaking is concerned, she uses debates and open-ended questions, creates dialogs with new vocabulary, implements projects in class where students need to negotiate, and employs picture descriptions also in connection with students' opinions. She often uses brainstorming before any activity and new class topic, and pair or small group discussions.

As far as developing Helena's knowledge of her profession, she said that there were some opportunities she took advantage of, but they had to be during weekends as she cannot attend a conference at the expense of teaching during the week. There are many conferences organized by publishers that have a more commercial dimension, but she does not attend those too often. Helena had an opportunity to go to Malta for a workshop with some students, and it was fantastic. She shared and exchanged ideas with other English teachers from different European countries about additional materials and activities that could be used in teaching English. She enjoys working in groups on projects and tries to incorporate mini-projects in her classes as well, so students can learn to communicate and cooperate not only in the classroom, but also in the world outside after they finish high school. For example, she gives students posters, and they are supposed to work together in groups to write down the advantages and disadvantages of living in a city or a village. Another time, also in groups, students were supposed to write a story containing as many newly learned words and grammatical structures as they could.

As far as multiple-choice tests are concerned, Helena does not let her students guess the answer. Rather, her students must justify their choices for the correct answer and provide logical explanations as to why all the other answers are not correct. Multiple-choice parts are always incorporated into the final English exams, thus Helena does many such tests with her students because she wants her students to feel comfortable and prepared at the final exams. However, if it were up to her, she would use multiple-choice tests only as a form of review, not as extensive parts of lessons.

If Helena met a new teacher who just started her/his career, she would tell her/him that it was important to have passion for teaching English, otherwise it would very hard and challenging. There is a lot of bureaucracy besides teaching, which is unmotivating. There are constant changes of rules about how to teach and how to conduct the exams, and it is hard to work out a solid system because the reality changes with every new school year. Helena would advise them how important it is to be flexible, otherwise, it creates frustration. However, despite the adversities, it is important to be a friendly but demanding teacher, to be human and understanding towards students, but also be firm and established in your own principles. It is important to be diligent and meticulous, and to never make a student cry. Helena remembers when she was a young student, when students were treated as numbers and passive receivers of knowledge, whose opinions did not matter. It is so much better now, when students' voices count.

When answering the question about what Helena finds difficult is being a teacher she says she does not like bureaucracy. She loves teaching and she loves the youth in the school that is willing to learn, but bureaucracy is something that can discourage her passion for teaching. There are too many administrative, organizational, and secretarial duties coming from school authorities and the Ministry of Education, which the English teachers are obligated to perform.

Helena does not remember particular methods she learned during her university studies but she does not consider it important as through years of experimenting she sees what works and what does not in her classes. She believes that using one method would not be appropriate for students anyway, as it would lead to students' boredom, routine and monotony in the classroom. She believes in a diversity of activities and that lessons should be interactive, involving plenty of opportunities for students to speak, and connect with their interests and the reality surrounding them, involving authentic materials, realia, images, and technology.

Classroom Observations

From the middle of February to the middle of May 2015, I observed Helena in her classroom. Helena does not have her own EFL classroom. She teaches in a few different classrooms, which she finds challenging, as she often has to move her teaching materials and her equipment from one classroom to another. She was observed teaching in two different classrooms. One was very small where only about 17 students fit. It was painted dark yellow and had two windows. The other classroom was a big computer room where easily 30 students could fit. The room was equipped with 17 computers and an interactive board.

Helena used English as the language of instruction for most of the time except for clarifications. She represents the British English version. Students were expected to respond in English most of the time as well. When the students used Polish they were redirected by Helena to speak English. Helena had her students answer verbally in English by providing opportunities for all students to speak English during classes.

During one class, the students were practicing a grammatical structure, the Passive Voice. Helena divided her students into pairs in order to practice the Passive Voice. They were asked to talk about occurrences that took place in the students' lives during the last or this week. For example, one student said, "Beata's laundry was done on Tuesday," "Stefan's dog was given food and water a few hours ago," and "A birthday gift has been given to Karina's mom this morning." During the paired activity, students were able to learn grammar in context and practice it in connection with real life situations while developing their speaking, communicative, and cooperative skills.

During another class, students talked about art, one of the topics required to be reviewed for the final oral exam of English. Using a whiteboard, Helena drew a chart containing various branches of art, such as painting and sculpting. She made sure the students understood the vocabulary, and she provided descriptive definitions of the new words. Sometimes she would draw a picture to explain a new word. For instance, for 'still-life' she drew a picture of a basket of fruit on a table. Then the students were asked to participate in a discussion on the topic of art. Helena stimulated her students by asking questions such as, "Can everyone be an artist or is a special talent needed to be an artist?" and "Define art – is street art true art?" Next, Helena gave each pair of students a picture representing a piece of modern art, and the students working with their elbow partners were asked to discuss if the given piece was a true piece of art to them, and why or why not. Helena then asked some pairs to share their arguments. After, Helena provided images of different types of artistic architecture. Each pair received an image of a castle, and they had to describe it to their partner, and then share a story about a castle they had visited in the past.

This activity connected with the reality of Helena's students' lives, as there are numerous old castles in Poland and surely each student had visited at least one in the past. The activity provided students the opportunity to express their thoughts and ideas, and to connect with the real world of art. It also provided them opportunities to practice their speaking, communicative, argumentative, and cooperative skills while working with their elbow partners. Additionally, these students learned new content information on the topic of art through the means of the English language.

When learning new vocabulary associated with the theme of feelings and emotions, Helena introduced the topic of happiness. She asked her students to think and share in pairs what made them happy. Then the students were encouraged to share their ideas on happiness with the whole class. By being provided the opportunity to prepare ideas on the topic of happiness in pairs, the students avoided the stress if they were selected by Helena to answer directly in front of the whole class.

Next, Helena presented a picture of an African couple. The students had to describe the picture and express how the people might feel. Helena connected the content of the picture with real life situations and with what her students had to say about relationships and their relationship experiences. Helena drew a mind map and, relying on her students' previous knowledge, asked them to brainstorm vocabulary concerning relationship collocations. The class and Helena came up with terms such as: one-sided love, love at first sight, to fall in love, to propose and such. Also, unpleasant but associated with the reality of the students' negative feelings, they came up with: to be rejected, to breakup, to cheat, to be unfaithful and so on. Then the students listened to the story of a relationship between two refugees from Africa.

One student mentioned the movie *Hotel Rwanda*, and the other students were able to discuss it and make a connection between the lesson in the story and the movie. The students were then asked to sit in a circle, and using their own words, they were asked to retell the story. Each student had to say one sentence until the story was told. The students were required to use sequencing vocabulary such as: as first, at the beginning, then, next, finally, at last, and such. This activity provided the students a chance to practice their speaking, communicative, and cooperative skills. They also learned new vocabulary; practiced sequencing vocabulary; shared their own personal stories, feelings, and emotions; and identified themselves within the content of the class by connecting to real life situations.

Continuing with the theme of feeling and emotions, Helena kept in mind her students' oral portion of the final exam in English, and often provided her students with opportunities to practice in the format of the exam. One of the exam requirements is to describe a picture. Thus, she provided a picture of two girls crying, supposedly with joy. Using vocabulary from the previous lesson concerning emotions and feelings, students were asked to describe the picture individually using new idiomatic expressions such as: "over the moon," "with flying colors," and "have butterflies in one's stomach." The students used the Simple Present and Present Continuous Tenses. They were asked to use their imagination and to speculate why the girls were crying. Then the students shared their ideas with the whole class. It was crucial that the students described the picture answering questions starting with who, what, and why, as well as give details about the feelings and emotions of the people in the image. In this way, students were able to experience the authentic feeling of the final oral exam. Helena made sure all the students had opportunities to say at least one sentence and practice their speaking skills in this way.

This activity enabled the students to practice for the final oral exam, practice present tenses, use new vocabulary from multiple lessons, and use their speaking skills. Through practicing their imaginative and speculative skills the students were able to express their personal ideas, opinions, and thoughts in English.

Helena often asked her students to prepare speeches on a topic associated with a given theme of a class, as this activity was part of the final oral exam. During one class a student presented a speech entitled, "Pros and cons of being a child of a celebrity." First, the student talked about it in small groups and then all the students were involved in the debate. The students who saw the pros of the situation sat on the right side of the classroom, and the students who saw the cons sat on the left side. This activity provided the students an opportunity to practice for the final exams, since during the actual exam they would receive a topic to develop. The students were also able to practice their speaking, debating, and argumentative skills, and connect their thoughts and ideas with the real world and the situations of actual celebrities the students knew about.

During one lesson, the students read a text about Wayne Gretzky, a Canadian hockey player. Since Gretzky's last name sounds Polish, the students were interested about his roots and researched about him on the Internet. Unfortunately, they were not able to find a Polish connection. Helena connected Wayne Gretzky's story with sports the students liked and also participated in. She also asked her students about their favorite female and male sport champions and models, and why they chose them. The students mentioned Polish sportsmen, such as a martial arts champion, Mariusz Pudzianowski, and a boxing champion, Andrzej Gołota. Through the discussion the students were able to practice their speaking skills and connect to their sports interests in their native Poland and the world.

During one observation, Helena introduced the topic of natural disasters. First, she asked the students to brainstorm vocabulary about natural and ecological disasters. Then she asked the students to write the vocabulary on the whiteboard. They came up with vocabulary such as; volcano, hurricane, earthquake, tsunami, forest fire, flood, drought, and such. If the students did not know a particular word, the student who mentioned the word was asked to provide a definition in English. Helena then divided the students into pairs and asked them to think and share the effects of each type of the disaster. Next, the students shared what they thought in English with the whole class. Helena selected particular students for answers, thus all the students had opportunities to share their ideas.

Following this, Helena played a video about disasters in the world. With images and sounds, the students were able to practice most of the vocabulary that was mentioned during the brainstorming activity. They were also able to learn new vocabulary from the video. Whenever a new word associated with a disaster was mentioned, Helena stopped the video for the students to learn it. She tried to explain a given word by associating the images in the video and provided hints so the students were able to figure out its meaning of the new word. In this way, the students learned such words as landslide, radioactive leakage, greenhouse effect, hole in the ozone layer, and debris-rubble. Through the pair activity, students were able to practice their speaking, communicative, and cooperative skills. Through brainstorming and sharing information on the vocabulary and the use of moving images and sounds, students also practiced their thinking skills in English and broadened their vocabulary on a topic, which although unpleasant, was important, as it connected with the world's reality.

Helena demonstrated that teaching was about students, not about teacher. Her lessons were creative where students' ideas mattered. She showed the importance of interactive education and that fact that fun in learning English is crucial by using e.g. games. Helena also provided evidence that the use of authentic materials and technology were equally significant in the process of teaching and learning English in the classroom.

Textbooks Helena uses for teaching EFL are:
- McKinley, S. Hastings, B., & Raczyńska, R. (2012). *New matura success*. Warszawa, Poland: Longman/Pearson.
- Umińska, M., Hastings, B., Chandler, D., Fricker, R., & Trapnell, B. (2014). *English: Repetytorium maturalne*. Warszawa, Poland: Longman/Pearson.

Portrait of Participant Four: Lidia

Interviews

Lidia possesses Master's degree in teaching English as a foreign language. She has had a high school teaching experience of 11 years. Lidia's fascination with

English started in childhood when her brother bought her some comics in English. She was in second grade then, in 1992. Lidia's mother was an elementary school teacher, and that contributed to the fact Lidia wanted to be a teacher as well, a teacher of English in particular. Her parents saw her interest in English, and thus enrolled her in private lessons of English, as she only had French in elementary school. The English teacher under whom Lidia studied taught in a very traditional way. There was a lot of memorization of vocabulary and irregular verbs. There were drills and repetitions and no games at all. The teacher stressed pronunciation and even shouted at the students if there was something she did not approve of the students did. The textbook was very traditional, focusing mainly on grammar, and it had no pictures at all.

Lidia started high school in 1998. The class was divided into two groups regardless of students' proficiency in English. There were about 17 students in each group. The approach was different; there was more stress on speaking skills and answering questions concerning opinions, or questions such as, "What would you do if...?" Lidia found it difficult, as she did not have much practice with speaking English. She was used to passive learning, where she was never asked about her opinions in English. There was a lot of grammar as well, but she was used to that, so it was her comfort zone. There was not much focus on learning or developing the listening skills of students.

In high school, the textbook was more progressive. They were focused on the development of all four literacy skills: listening, reading, speaking, and writing. The texts were interesting. She remembers two particular texts, one about chewing gum and the other Coca-Cola. Lidia felt that the textbooks were more about the world, connecting with students' interests in the American culture. Even though grammar was still important, it was not taught in isolation and was connected to the four skills through various listening, reading, writing, and speaking exercises. Grammar was taught in context. Sometimes students had to connect their thoughts and ideas with a given grammatical structure. The teacher incorporated students' feelings, emotions, and identities into teaching English.

After graduating from high school, Lidia was admitted to university to become a teacher of English. At the university, all the courses were in English, but Lidia did not have difficulties with understanding them. Speaking English was still difficult for her, especially because there were peers who she felt had a broader knowledge of oral English than she did at that time. Lidia had Polish and native English-speaking professors. The Polish professors were theoreticians; they taught methodology and other subjects in the form of very traditional lectures. Vocabulary and conversations were with native speaking teachers, who were more progressive in their teaching strategies. They used presentations, dialogs, debates, and pair and group work activities. It was more interesting for Lidia and other students. This type of active learning was stressful for Lidia at the beginning, but then she got used to it, especially that neither Polish teachers, nor native speakers of English corrected students' mistakes in English.

Lidia enjoyed methodology classes where she learned various games to play with future students while teaching English. She also liked the idea that she and other students often played the roles of future students while learning various interactive activities. Lidia thought it was very important to learn these new strategies, so she could understand her future students better and have more empathy towards them and their challenges of learning English. After Lidia graduated from the university, she started working in the high school she has been working at since 2004.

Lidia noticed a difference between native English-speaking teachers from the United States and the Polish teachers at her university. The American teachers were more focused on conversation, interaction, and communication, and they created a friendly atmosphere allowing students to open up and not to be afraid to speak English. The Polish teachers were very strict and conservative, and students felt the distance between the teachers and themselves. The students also felt stress in the classes of the Polish teachers' classes.

Answering the question of how Lidia teaches, she responded, "I use different methods. I don't even remember their theoretical models per se, because I don't think it is important. What is important is a variety of different teaching approaches and activities to avoid boredom and monotony, and to develop all the four skills equally." Lidia tries to connect teaching, for example grammar, with real life situations. She admits she sometimes provides a lecture on a given grammatical issue, but then she always uses some activities to make the theory more real. The students like to have information in their notebooks on the rules of the English language. It gives them a sense of structure and predictability. Lidia also uses a Communicative Approach where students have opportunities to practice given grammatical structures through skits and dialogs. The textbook and the textbook CDs are saturated with interesting exercises in which students can practice grammar.

Lidia uses warm-up activities and always connects with students' interests and issues associated with their lives. She also has discussions and debates with her students, during which they have opportunities to practice vocabulary from a given area, agree or disagree, and express their opinions, feelings, and emotions. Debates are more difficult, especially for younger students who have a lower level of English. Lidia tries to reach her students and go beyond the four walls of the classroom and connect the content material with her students' realities.

As far as TPSI group configurations are concerned, Lidia more often uses pair work than small groups. Students like working in pairs because they feel less stressed than when talking in front of the whole class. In small groups, it is often one student that is a leader who takes over the group, and the rest of the students do not necessarily work together. Therefore, it is important that Lidia walks around the classroom and checks the groups' progress. "Pair work is crucial, as students need to work on their speaking, communicative, and cooperative skills," she said.

Another important aspect of teaching and learning is the incorporation of technology. Present generations of students grew up using computers, the Internet, and other technological devices. They feel comfortable and enjoy using them in everyday life. Therefore, Lidia believes it is crucial to integrate technology as a significant part of education. Using technology, students have opportunities to learn through means that are appealing and exciting to them, which makes the educational process more pleasant and interesting to students. Besides the above-mentioned videos, movies, and other online materials, Lidia uses an online dictionary. As a result of visualizing and listening to the pronunciation, students remember new words more easily and more permanently.

Answering the question concerning the development of speaking skills, Lidia said that in order to develop her students' speaking skills, she used activities that were frequently used during the final oral exam. These are warm-up questions, picture descriptions, asking about advantages and disadvantages of some situations, all of which teaches students logical thinking, critical thinking, speaking skills, and making connections between content knowledge and students' lives and experiences.

As far as picture description is concerned, Lidia tries to prepare her students not only to be fluent in English but also to think and speak maturely, because the pictures the students are asked to describe and reflect on are difficult to describe, even in Polish. For instance, a student was asked to describe a vase in a baby cot and reflect on what the connection might be. Lidia does not like these types of pictures for students to describe, because students without a broad amount of vocabulary are not able to demonstrate their speaking skills in English, as they do not know what to say even in Polish, not to mention in English. According to Lidia and other English teachers, these types of picture exercises do not seem to reflect students' genuine knowledge of the English language and do not check what students know and are able to say in English.

As mentioned above, Lidia also uses discussions, debates, dialogs, and conversations to develop her students' speaking skills. Speeches are also popular, but with older students who are more proficient in English and have better skills to produce coherent speeches. The students need to be mature in order to produce speeches. Lidia conducts mock oral final exams of English. She takes questions from previous years and practices with one student and exam set at a time, so that the student has a feeling of the one-to-one exam and is better emotionally and mentally prepared for the actual exam.

Lidia has her opinion on games and thinks, "...games are important in teaching English, because fun is important in the process of learning. Students' favorite is *Shark*." She draws a picture of a shark in the ocean and stairs going down to the shark. It is similar to *Hangman*. Each letter of a word that is not guessed means the player moves down one stair toward the shark. Another game is where students have to think about a famous person and provide three words describing the person. The rest of the students have to guess who the person is by asking "Yes" and "No" questions. Another form of fun is when students act as teachers and grade each other's mock mini vocabulary tests. They do these activities especially before holidays and summer vacations when students are already enjoying free time in their minds, and they are not able to focus on serious schoolwork anymore.

Another form of fun, especially when the students are tired at the end of the school day, is the incorporation of music with learning. A student prepares a song that is popular among students, distributes copies of the lyrics obtained from the Internet with missing vocabulary the students probably do not know. While listening to the song, students identify the words and write them down. If the vocabulary is too challenging, the student who prepared the song has to be prepared to provide the definition of the word. In the rush towards final exam preparations, the competition of raising schools' statistics, which students feel and are negatively influenced by, fun in forms of games is very important, as Lidia's sees her role as a teacher who encourages students to learn English.

In order to create a more interesting and authentic environment for learning English, Lidia realizes the importance of using genuine materials, not only videos and movies, but also authentic articles, newspaper clips, and other reading materials. She also watches the news in English with her students, for example, Sky News or BBC News, so that students are updated about what is going on in the English-speaking world and the world in general through the lenses of the English language. Lidia admits it is not easy to incorporate additional materials because there is always the rush for the exams, and it takes time for her at home to prepare lessons with authentic materials, which is challenging with her two young children.

When holidays come, such as St. Patrick's Day or Christmas, Lidia always tries to celebrate the days by reading authentic articles, doing crosswords, and other fun activities, so that students also have a more realistic feeling of what it means to live in an English-speaking country. Their textbooks have some information about cultural, political, educational, and governmental aspects of Great Britain and sometimes the United States as well, so students also have a more authentic process of learning the English language. Lidia tries to broaden what is in the textbook if time allows.

Lidia also is an enthusiast of projects, role-plays, skits, and theater with her students, because through these activities, students are entertained, and they improve their English without even knowing it. However, these activities are time and energy consuming, and limited by lack of time as the bureaucratic priority is placed in preparation for the final exams. Lidia does mini-projects with students where they need to brainstorm ideas, speak to each other, communicate, and cooperate. Unfortunately, there are no funds for posters, jumbo sticky notes, and markers, so students often use their own notebooks, which takes away a bit of the spirit of team work in small groups.

Lidia said that from her perspective, her model of teaching has changed. When she started teaching in 2004, she thought teaching grammar was more important than anything else. Today, she thinks that developing speaking, communicative, and cooperative skills is more important than grammar, but she still has to teach a lot of grammar because it will be present on the final oral and written exams of English. However, Lidia now tries to teach grammar in a more interesting way through personal examples and exercises that connect to students and build their literacy identities, interests, and relevance to real life situations. The development of speaking skills is crucial because if students do not practice using vocabulary, they forget even the simplest, most basic words.

As far as gaining more professional qualifications and knowledge in the field is concerned, Lidia mentioned that she occasionally goes to conferences and workshops. However, if they are organized during a weekday, she cannot attend, as the school does not allow teachers to miss classes. Weekends are difficult too, as Lidia wants to spend time with her husband and her two young children. Sometimes publishing companies organize workshops, but they usually have a very commercial purpose, which is to sell textbooks, thus Lidia does not think they are worth attending, especially for experienced English teachers such as herself.

However, Lidia attended a couple of international workshops, one in Finland and one in Italy, with some of her students, where she was able to exchange ideas with teachers from other countries, which she found enriching to her own teaching practice. Lidia also pointed out the benefit of students going along with her to the workshops, as they were able to present their skills in exchanges with students and teachers from other countries. Since the means of communication in these environments was the English language, the students had natural opportunities to practice their speaking, communicative, and cooperative skills.

Answering the question of how Lidia would advise new teachers of English, she said that new teachers could not forget how it felt to be a student. They need to have empathy and understanding on one hand, but on the other, there needs to be a mutual respect. Students must know where the line is and not cross it. New teachers also have to see students individually and as a specific group, and their different needs. Additionally, a new teacher needs to put energy into making lessons appealing and interesting so students are engaged and a connection between teacher and students is built. A teacher must also reflect on if he/she really has a vocation to teach, because it is hard, not only to teach, but also to perform numerous activities that come with the profession of a teacher. There are people who are teachers only because they like the subject, like biology, math, or English. This is not the same as having a vocation to be a teacher and to desire to work with youth, school authorities, and educational structures.

In terms of teaching methods, Lidia does not recall particular methods or models, but she does not find it important because she would not use one method anyway, as it would be too much of a routine and a monotony for the students. Through her years and experience, Lidia has been improving her ways of teaching to create conditions that would optimally increase her students' English language skills. As Lidia mentioned before, she initially imitated her own teachers and professors, yet through the years she has been changing and adding activities that contribute to her students' success in their process of learning English.

Classroom Observations

From the middle of February to the middle of May 2015, I observed Lidia in her classroom. Lidia does not have her own EFL classroom, and rather teaches in a few different ones. She finds it challenging, as she often has to move her teaching materials and her equipment from classroom to classroom. She was observed teaching in two different classrooms. One is very small where only about 15–17 students could fit, painted dark yellow with two windows. The walls in the classroom are decorated with maps of the United Kingdom, the United States, and Canada. The other classroom is big, sunny and painted yellow with big windows. The walls are decorated with a map of the United Kingdom of Great Britain and Northern Ireland and posters of popular traveling places in London. The EFL room is equipped with a whiteboard.

Lidia spoke English with a British accent, used British vocabulary, and British grammar all the time in the class, and if students responded in Polish, they were redirected to speak English as well. Only on special occasions to avoid misunderstandings was the Polish language used in the classes. During all the observed classes, whenever the students were assigned activities to perform, Lidia was walking around, helping, advising, answering questions, and checking students' work in order for them to perform the activities successfully.

During the first observed class, the topic of the lesson was feelings and happiness. First, keeping in mind the importance of practice for the final oral exam, Lidia showed a picture of two angry people to her students. Lidia then selected students to describe possible feelings of the individuals in the picture, how they felt and why. The students were encouraged to use their imagination and to speculate.

Then, Lidia connected the topic of feelings with real life situations, and thus students were able to relate the topic of the lesson to their own lives and identities. They were asked to share situations when they felt angry or happy, and why. Knowing that one student loved and rode horses, Lidia asked her to connect the topic of feeling and happiness to her love for horses. During the same class, Lidia showed a few more pictures to the students. Then she divided the students into pairs and gave them a choice to select a pictures to describe. One of the pictures presented was a winner of a marathon bursting with joy.

These activities provided the students with an opportunity to use their speaking skills, practice for the final oral exam, use their imaginative and speculative skills, and connect with their real feelings and life situations. The pair activity gave the students opportunities to practice their communicative and cooperative skills. The students were also in an environment where they felt their opinions and feelings mattered, and that they were listened to.

Lidia used the whiteboard to explain new vocabulary and to make sure students knew the correct spelling. She provided synonyms of a given word and descriptive definitions, all in English. Lidia relied on her students' previous knowledge, and she prompted them for collocations, synonyms, and antonyms to practice new vocabulary. For example, when Lidia asked her students about the meaning of the word 'dreadful,' she heard synonyms such as 'terrible' and 'awful,' and antonyms such as 'nice' and 'pleasant.' Through this activity, the students were able to broaden their vocabulary and practice their brainstorming and speaking skills.

During one observation, the topic of the lesson was communication. The students were free to disagree with any point of the lesson, as long as they expressed their opinions in English, which developed into a productive debate in class. One of the questions Lidia asked was: "In the era of cellphones, should landlines be in existence?" Next, Lidia presented a few pictures of communication devices. The students were divided in pairs and asked to select one device they thought was the least useful and talk about it with a partner. Afterwards, they presented their choices and arguments to the whole class. Many students selected a fax machine as the least useful. The students were able to debate for a few minutes about the technological devices, monitored by Lidia.

The lesson on communication provided the students an opportunity to practice their speaking, communicative, cooperative, argumentative, and debating skills. The students were also able to connect the topic of the lesson to their everyday reality and the presence of technology in their lives. Technology has been a part of students' lives from the moment they were born, something the new generation of young people is very much interested in and comfortable with.

During another observation, for the purpose of practicing for the final oral exam, Lidia began the lesson by presenting a picture to her students that represented the stressful situation of going to a dentist. The students needed to describe the picture and connect it with their own personal feelings, emotions, and opinions they had when they went to their dentists. Lidia prompted her students with questions such as "Do you like going to the dentist, why/why not?" And "Do you find it stressful, why/why not?"

Next, Lidia divided the students into pairs and provided them with seven pictures concerning human feelings and emotions in stressful situations. Each student was supposed to choose one picture that she/he found to be the most stressful, and justify this choice to her or his elbow partner. Volunteers and selected students then presented their choices and arguments to the whole class.

Through these activities, students were able to practice their speaking skills, to connect with the reality of their own dental care, and to express in pairs their own feelings and emotions when under pressure or feeling stress. Through the activity, the students were also able to practice their speaking, communicative, and cooperative skills.

During the next observed class, the topic of the lesson was food. The students learned vocabulary associated with various types of eaters: vegetarians, vegans, fruitarians, and raw foodists. Relying on her students' previous knowledge and by providing definitions in English and drawing pictures on the whiteboard, Lidia taught them new vocabulary concerning these types of eaters. Lidia personalized the topic of food by asking her students what type of eaters they were, and what kind of food they ate, connecting food and their realities. Next, the students worked in pairs with their elbow partners. They were assigned one type of eater, and they had to prepare a dish for that type.

They were allowed to use electronic devices, such as cell phones and tablets, to look for recipes in English. The pair activity enabled the students to practice their speaking, communicative, and cooperative skills, and they were able to connect the topic of the lesson to the reality of their own food choices. They were able to use their imaginative skills when they were asked to create meals based on recipes through the means of technological devices.

Next, Lidia organized a class debate. The topic of the debate was: "What are the reasons for eating and not eating meat?" According to preference, students were asked to join the pro-meat-eating group or the anti-meat-eating group. Each of the two groups was asked to provide several points in the form of bullet on a provided poster. The students from each group monitored by Lidia debated back and forth. She made sure each of the students participated in the debate. Through the activity, students were able to practice their speaking, logical thinking, communicative, cooperative, argumentative, interactive, and debating skills, and connect the topic with the global issue of eating and not eating certain foods in the world.

Later, Lidia connected the topic of food to a different dimension of food. She presented some pictures of people living in poverty in Africa. She prompted her students to think and talk about the problem of world hunger, and what emotions and feelings the topic brought out of the students. Through the discussion, the students were able to practice their thinking and speaking skills. They were able to connect the topic of the lesson with the real problem of global hunger, and broaden their knowledge and express their empathy, feelings, and emotions on the matter.

During another class, the students read a text on shopping malls. Lidia used pictures accompanying the text to practice for the final oral exam, which showed young people in a shopping mall. Next, Lidia asked a question for students to discuss in pairs: "Do teenagers like to hang out in shopping malls? If yes justify, if not, justify as well." Then the students shared their ideas with the whole class.

Lidia then divided the class into two groups. One of the groups prepared arguments supporting the idea of building shopping malls, and the other group prepared arguments against the idea. Next, the debate, started monitored by Lidia. The two activities enabled the students to practice their speaking, communicative, cooperative, argumentative, and debating skills. The students were also able to connect the class topic to their own reality if teenagers spend time hanging out in shopping malls.

The topic of the next class was on jobs and employment, on issue the students were interested in as they would be looking for part-time and full-time employment after high school graduation. Lidia presented some pictures concerning jobs. Working in pairs, students were asked to choose a picture of a job that required the most qualifications and explain why. Next, Lidia asked another question: "Which job is a dead end job to you, and which is rewarding? Justify your choices."

To practice for the oral exam, Lidia then divided the class into two groups and provided each with a quotation about jobs. One group received the quote, "I would rather be a happy dustman than an unhappy millionaire," and the other group received the quote, "It doesn't matter what job you do. It is how you do it." First, the pairs in a given group were asked to provide three arguments supporting their quote, and then each group (using bullets) was required to provide the five best arguments for the assigned quote. The groups then shared their arguments with the whole class. The pair and group activities transformed into a whole class discussion, where each student was encouraged to participate.

These activities provided students opportunities to practice their speaking, communicative, cooperative, argumentative, and debating skills. They were also able to connect the topic of the lesson to their own reality as young people facing the issue of looking for a job in the near future and to see that their voices and opinions mattered.

The last observed class was devoted to a medical topic. Lidia started with a final oral exam practice. The students were divided into pairs and had to improvise doctor-patient dialogs in a doctor's office, without any previous preparation. The dialogs were supposed to be about five-minutes long. One student acted as a doctor/examiner and the other as a patient/examinee. Next, selected pairs re-enacted these conversations in front of the whole class. Lidia created a whole class discussion by asking questions such as: "What are doctors' responsibilities and consequences of being a doctor?" "Do you believe in natural medicine, why/why not? Justify your opinion." "Is being a doctor popular in Poland? Why/why not? Justify your opinion." "What do you know about the situation of doctors in Poland?" "What are the advantages, disadvantages, and dangers of being medically self-informed via the Internet?"

During the last observed class, the students were able to practice their speaking, communicative, cooperative, argumentative, and interactive skills in an authentic like environment of the actual oral exam. They were able to express their thoughts and opinions. They were also able to broaden their knowledge and vocabulary concerning the medical field and to connect to its contemporary reality of the medical field, outside of the four classroom walls.

Lidia believes that education is about students, not about teachers and it is important student see the connection between their realities, experiences, hobbies, interests, and the content materials. The connection is what keeps students motivated to study and makes them interested in the English language.

Textbooks Lidia uses for teaching EFL are:

– Evans, V., & Dooley, J. (2007). *Upstream intermediate*. Newbury Berkshire, UK: Express.
– Umińska, M., Hastings, B., Chandler, D., Fricker, R., & Trapnell, B. (2014). *English: Repetytorium maturalne*. Warszawa, Poland: Longman/Pearson.

Portrait of Participant Five: Maria

Interviews

Maria has Master's degree in teaching English. She has been an EFL high school teacher for the last 23 years. She started learning English in the fifth grade in 1978. She did not study English in school; she attended private lessons given by a Catholic nun. The teaching was very grammar and translation-based, had a lot of grammatical exercises done one by one, had almost no opportunities for students to speak English, and had no revision of vocabulary. It was a very traditional, passive, and old-fashioned way of learning twice a week in a group of eight students. The textbooks had almost no pictures, just grammatical exercises. The teacher spoke Polish all the time to her students.

Maria started high school in 1982. She was accepted to an English language extended class and had seven hours of English per week, which was intense for high schools in Poland. The textbooks were a bit more modern than the textbooks Maria used while attending her private lessons of English. The teacher also had a more progressive methodology of teaching, which was not like it is today, but still modern for the 1980s Poland. It was then that Maria realized there was a better and more interesting way of learning English. It was revolutionary in comparison to the private lessons Maria had experienced. In high school, there was speaking English and practicing pronunciation. If any grammatical or vocabulary element was introduced, it was revised using the four literacy skills: listening, speaking, reading, and writing. There were speeches, skits, drama, and theater, and the teacher spoke English most of the time. The learning was active and creative. The teaching reached beyond the four walls of the classroom, as the teacher had access to authentic materials from Great Britain, which was not common in communist Poland in the 1980s.

After Maria graduated from high school, she decided to become a teacher of the English language, influenced by her high school English teacher and relatives who were teachers as well. She attended university to become a teacher of English. She studied methodology in forms of lectures only. However, there was no practical methodology that she learned. She considers that the university did not prepare her to teach in school.

After Maria finished her studies, she became an English teacher. She had already been giving individual private lessons in English, and taught some private courses in small groups, which is how she was creating her own methodology of teaching English as a foreign language. It was a trial and error method, and she drew conclusions from her own teaching methodology. First, she worked in a private elementary school teaching English to young children, which was the year of experimentation. As Maria had the same type of classes, she taught the same material six times. With every group she improved her methodology. The first group was the most difficult and challenging and the sixth was the easiest, as every next class after the first went under modification. The textbooks were more advanced in comparison to the textbooks from which Maria was learning. They had images in them, and the strategies they proposed were more appealing and more interesting to students. They had listening materials as well. This was around 1993.

After a year, Maria took a full time position teaching high school English, and she has been teaching there ever since. She decided she needed to be demanding of her students, but she needed to be human with them and understanding as well. She had a time in her teaching career when she was giving her students a lot of short tests. Then she decided it was not very good, as it was more a verification of students' knowledge than of teaching and learning. Maria decided to speak in English as much as possible and to speak to students from the very beginning, except when explaining grammatical issues, as she noticed that explaining an abstract issue in a foreign language was useless, especially with less advanced students. Sometimes the issue was difficult for students to understand, even in their native language of Polish, not to mention in English. The more advanced the groups, the more Maria spoke English.

Maria sees the need of making her classes more authentic, reaching outside of the four walls of the classroom. She does English theater shows with her students. She holds mock courtroom trials where her students have opportunities to practice previously introduced English vocabulary associated with the judicial system. Frequently, students write their own scripts for plays. Maria's students used to buy magazines in English and she used to work on articles with her students in class, but since the era of the Internet, Maria uses authentic online articles that she interprets and analyzes in terms of grammar and vocabulary, then turns them into discussions with the students so they can practice their logic, thinking, and speaking skills. Sometimes Maria watches video clips, movies, or parts of movies with her students, and then has discussions and debates with them. Students often watch and read in English on their own time and often will bring information about shows, movies, programs, and news to the class to share with everyone. Sometimes Maria thinks the students know more about what is going on in the English-speaking world than she does.

Maria admits she likes using authentic materials with her students but wishes she had more time to use them. Unfortunately, the list of themes she has to cover with her students to prepare them for the final exams is long, and there is never enough time to do things with her students that would connect more to the English-speaking world. She feels she had more autonomy to teach in the past, and now there is such a strong pressure to prepare students for the final exams, which represents a testing philosophy. In the past, Maria taught English, and then the students had to demonstrate what they learned at the end of high school. Today, it is teaching and learning in preparation for the final exams. Most of the exercises and tasks are constructed as if they were final exam exercises and tasks. Maria feels it kills teacher and student creativity and individuality, and produces students as test-takers and test-solvers. She feels suffocated by the system of 'test taking slavery,' as she put it. However, she is satisfied with contemporary textbooks that have more cultural, political, geographical, and historical aspects about the United Kingdom and the United States than ever before. Some readings in the textbooks are reprinted authentic materials.

Answering the question of how Maria develops her students' speaking skills, she responded that speaking is crucial in her teaching philosophy. She explains from the very beginning that students will have to speak and talk a lot in her classes. Students are motivated to prepare dialogs, speeches, presentations, screenplays, role-plays, and interviews based on some of the proposed themes in the textbook. For example, the students mock a BBC or CNN interview in connection with practicing the Passive Voice grammatical structure. Students need to prepare new vocabulary and share it with the rest of the students. For instance, if a given textbook unit is about education, then Maria expands it to the topic of truancy, and the students discuss it. When speaking, Maria considers the communicative role of the English language as the most important skill, thus she does not correct grammatical mistakes while students speak. She does not want to stress her students either.

Maria makes sure every student has an opportunity to say something in the class, and that the newly learned vocabulary is utilized by students. Sometimes she asks for volunteers to answer questions, but often she selects students to speak and answer questions. Otherwise, some students would never open their mouths in the class at all.

Maria states that there needs to be a review of the vocabulary as students frequently forget. However, in other forms of exercises and practice, they have opportunities to retrieve vocabulary from their memory. It is always easier to recall a new word or phrase than learn something brand new. Students often work in teams of two when there is a debate (pros and cons) or groups, and then they have to 'sell' their knowledge to the rest of the class. Before any activity, brainstorming is important for students to think about a given topic. Maria finds it important for students to work in pairs, small groups, and teams, so they can interact, speak, communicate, and cooperate. However, she finds it challenging sometimes when working in TPSI group configurations, as students often switch to Polish. Though, many students use the opportunity to speak English as much as possible.

Students work in pairs when they, for example, describe pictures or create dialogs and interviews. Students work in small groups of three or four students when they work on projects with posters brainstorming ideas to create a final product. For example, when students work in small groups, they can write a summary together or bullet ideas, bring pros and cons of a topic together, and so forth. This is something that has changed in Maria's methodology, as previously, her teaching was more individualized, when students worked on their own.

Answering the question of how Maria's methodology has changed she responded, "...technology and the Internet really impacted the way of my teaching because there are numerous materials to teach English from." Technology brings the English-speaking world closer to the students, and the process of learning becomes more realistic to them. They know what they learn because they can use English in real life situations. They have friends all over the world, chatting with them via Skype in English. They will experience job interviews, and these days English is required for most of the jobs in Poland. They have opportunities to travel, as the Polish borders became open after the fall of communism. Maria organizes sightseeing trips and language camps to Great Britain for her students, and the students see that they can communicate well in a natural environment of the English language. The students see the purpose of learning English, and that it is not only an academic exercise. Maria also organizes workshops in other countries where the means of communication is English, and her students have opportunities to interact with other students and teachers from all over Europe where they can practice their speaking, communicative, and cooperative skills. The students learn how to feel comfortable in new environments and make new friends. It brings a lot of satisfaction to everyone.

Maria mentioned that trips to other countries contribute not only to students' learning but to her learning as well. In order to improve her qualifications and learn more methodologies, Maria attends locally organized conferences and workshops. The problem is that her high school does not give permission to attend any conferences or workshops at the expense of students' classes during a week. There are numerous workshops organized by publishing companies, but Maria does not consider them very valuable in the process of broadening her teaching knowledge, because their promotions of textbooks for teaching English are usually of a commercial character.

Maria considers using visuals important in the process of teaching English, as it enhances the process of learning and makes it more interesting for students. Therefore, she uses hard copy images, pictures, photographs, images from the Internet, PowerPoint presentations, and pictures from the textbooks, which often are connected with exemplary exercises for the final exams. Once, she even did a fashion show with her students. This is in addition to the already mentioned use of videos, YouTube clips, movies, and materials from the Internet that students bring as well.

In response to what Maria would advise new English teachers when coming to school to teach English, she said:

> Go through trial and error phase and put your own ideas into test. Unfortunately, everyone needs to learn from [their] own mistakes and errors. Besides, do not stress students out unnecessarily; create a friendly teaching and learning environment. Have an ability to admit your own mistakes and admit if you don't know an answer to students' questions. We are only humans who make human mistakes as well. If students are treated as humans, they will be empathetic and sympathetic to teachers as well.

Maria mentioned that obviously, there have to be boundaries and students need to do their work, but it is crucial that teachers listen to their students, and have the ability to negotiate with them, as they also have their weaknesses, dramas, problems, and may just feel under the weather. Student-centered pedagogy is highly desired.

Maria said that methodologically, new teachers are not advised to test their students too much. They should not give their students unannounced quizzes and tests. Education should be about quality learning and teaching, not about showing who has the power in the classroom, trying to catch students in what they do not know and give them bad grades. Teachers need to be in control of their classes and need to systematically check their students' knowledge, but it needs to be done in moderation.

Maria shared that once she was in charge of an intern, and during the comprehensive reading lesson, the intern asked the students about unknown vocabulary and grammatical constructions. She answered a couple of students' questions and considered the written text the students were working on as done. Maria advises new teachers to take each text into parts, ask students about synonyms of various words, and practice new constructions in new sentences with examples in context. Maria knows from her own experience that if only a few students ask questions, the majority are not familiar with all the new information in a new text. Each new learned item needs to be practiced in various ways, so the students can better remember the new material.

Sometimes it is important that teachers do fun stuff with their students, to make the process of learning English more pleasant. Therefore, Maria recommends games, theater, role-play, and drama be incorporated in the process of learning and teaching English. Students need to practice their speaking, communicative, interactive, and cooperative with each other, and they need to be creative – skills so needed in their future personal and professional lives.

As a final word, Maria mentioned that she loves teaching and she loves working with youth. Working with teenagers makes her feel young, but there is so much bureaucracy, rules, lack of time, and constant final exam preparations pressure that sometimes the loss of autonomy can be strongly and negatively influential on her positive spirit and passion for teaching English. A lot of the work Maria calls "paperology" needs to be done at home in front of a computer, which makes her feel that she is constantly working at the expense of spending time with her husband and two daughters.

Maria does not remember particular methods she learned during her university studies, but she believes that using one method would not be appropriate to students anyways, as it would lead to students' boredom, routine, and monotony in the classroom. She believes in using a variety of activities with her students, and that the lessons should be interactive, involving plenty of opportunities for students to speak, connecting students' interests and reality surrounding them, involving authentic materials, realia, images, and technology.

Classroom Observations

From the middle of February to the middle of May 2015, I observed Maria in her classroom. Maria has her own EFL classroom and teaches all her classes in the same classroom. The classroom is small, painted yellow with two windows. No more than 17 students fit in the room. The EFL classroom walls are decorated with flags of English-speaking countries such as Britain, United States, Canada, New Zealand, and Australia. There is also an impressive pencil sketched portrait of Queen Elizabeth II on the main wall, created by a student.

There are also pictures of students' and teachers' school exchange trips to Portugal, Austria, Germany, Italy, and Spain on the side walls. The EFL room is equipped with a whiteboard and a closet where Maria keeps her teaching materials, such as textbooks, dictionaries, and a CD player. The EFL room is neither equipped with computers, nor an interactive board.

Maria spoke English all the time. Her preference was British English with British pronunciation, vocabulary, and grammar. If students responded in Polish, she redirected them to English. The topic of the first observed lesson was, "Why the Antarctic is vital to our planet?" which was a title of a reading from a textbook. Beforehand, Maria asked her students to think, brainstorm, and research about the topic at home. The students were asked to prepare speeches in advance on the topic, connecting their research information and their opinions to the topic with the reality of the planet we live on. Maria selected three students to present their speeches. She made sure they presented, instead of just reading from a piece of paper. The presenting students were asked to write possible new vocabulary from their speeches with English definitions on the whiteboard. After the speeches a whole class discussion developed, monitored by Maria, who asked additional questions such as: "Why is the Antarctic key to the planet Earth?" and "What can an individual/government do to protect the environment?" This activity provided the students with an opportunity to practice their speaking skills (especially public speaking skills), learn new vocabulary, reflect on the natural environment they live in, and express their thoughts, opinions, and concerns about the topic.

Next, Maria connected the lesson topic to the final oral exam by presenting a picture of an iceberg to her students. In connection with the topic of the importance of the Antarctic to our planet, the students were asked to describe the picture and express their opinions. This activity gave an opportunity for students to practice their speaking skills, using newly acquired vocabulary from previous lessons, and to practice a picture description skill for their final oral exam.

During another class, the students had to present dialogs prepared in advance in pairs. The dialogs were about traveling to Tasmania and included new vocabulary from the previous classes on traveling. Maria selected three sets of pairs to present their dialogs in front of the whole class. The students were not allowed to read their dialogs, only present, to make the situation of traveling to Tasmania sound more natural and authentic. They practiced public speaking, a useful skill for the future. The pair work configuration activity provided students with opportunities to practice their communicative and cooperative skills, and to prepare a successful, authentic sounding dialog and to practice their speaking skills. Through the dialogs, the students were also able to review the new vocabulary and to consolidate it.

In one observed lesson, Maria devoted the class to the topic of family ties and relationships. She pointed to some pictures presenting families and family members in the students' textbooks. Maria gave students some time to discuss the pictures in pairs. Then the students were asked to share their ideas with the whole class. Next, she connected the topic to the ideas the students wanted to share about their own families, and a class discussion was developed.

As far as new vocabulary is concerned, Maria always relied on her students' prior knowledge, never underestimating that students might know a given word from the world around them, especially the Internet and movies, as movies in theaters in Poland are not dubbed and viewers usually read captions in Polish. If a given new word in English was not known to any of the students, Maria explained it using synonyms, antonyms, and descriptive definitions of the word.

Sometimes when teaching new vocabulary, Maria used a vocabulary extension technique. When students learned a new verb, for example "to long," Maria asked her students to provide an adjective of the verb and an adverb (longing-longingly). Through the use of visuals, the students had an opportunity to practice their speaking skills in preparation for their final oral exam. They were also able to use their communicative and cooperative skills when working with partners in pairs. The students were able to connect the topic of the lesson to their personal lives and in this way, have the sense of a more authentic English language learning environment as well.

During one class observation, it was the birthday of a student, and Maria incorporated the birthday celebration into the class. The students, along with Maria, sang the *Happy Birthday* song in English to the celebrated student. The unplanned activity helped to connect the English lesson with a real life situation, and identify the students with the reality surrounding them by using the English language.

Next, Maria checked her students' homework. They were supposed to watch the news in English on YouTube and then prepare their own news simulations. They were required to incorporate new vocabulary from the last few lessons. Maria pulled out a desk and a chair to imitate a news studio. She selected three students to present their work. She stressed on not reading from notes, but on speaking to make the news report sound as authentic as possible. The students used tablets and laptops to look professional in their news presentations.

When it came to new vocabulary the students might hear, the students presenting the news were responsible for preparing new words and phrases on the whiteboard, and then asking students about their meaning in English first. If any of the new vocabulary was unknown to any of the students, the presenting students explained it through the use of synonyms, antonyms, and/or definitions in English.

The Polish language was used only if absolutely necessary to understand crucial parts of the news simulations. The students focused on such authentic topics as terrorism, world health issues, and the world of science. After the news presentations, students were able to ask questions and comment on the issues.

This activity provided the students with opportunities to speak English in the class, become informed about world issues, and reflect, question, and discuss the presented topics in connection with the reality of the contemporary world. They were also able to practice vocabulary from the previous lessons and learn new vocabulary, as well as to practice and develop their English skills in an environment resembling an authentic environment of the English world.

In one classroom observation, Maria started with a warm-up activity. The previous night, the Polish movie *Ida* won an Oscar prize for the best foreign language movie (Pulver, 2015). Therefore, to connect to the English learning process, Maria opened up a discussion about the Oscar ceremony and the Polish movie. The activity gave students an opportunity to connect the English lesson with reality, and they could see that they could freely express their ideas and thoughts, and that their opinions mattered.

Connecting with the topic of *Ida*, about a young Catholic nun who left her convent to find her family, Maria offered a question for debate: "Should children over 18 move out from home? Agree or disagree." The students who saw the pros of the situation sat on the left side of the classroom, and the students who saw the cons sat on the right side of the classroom. Maria stressed the use of words associated with expressing opinions such as: I believe, in my opinion, I think, it seems to me that, to me, etc.

This activity provided the students an opportunity to practice for the final exams, since during the actual exam they would receive a topic to develop. The students were also able to practice their speaking, debating, argumentative skills, and connect their thoughts and ideas to the real world through the situations of actual celebrities the students knew about. The activity is evidence that language learning is not divided into teaching grammar or vocabulary only. Quite the contrary, students' learning can be contextualized in a more natural and an authentic environment of the English language.

Maria indicated the importance of student-centered pedagogy through motivating students to speak in English as much as possible, connecting reality to teaching and learning English, using various TPSI group configurations, projects (e.g. poster projects), doing fun stuff with her students, using authentic materials and technology in the classroom to make the process of learning of English more pleasant, and consequently more effective, efficient, and evident. Textbooks Maria uses for teaching EFL are:

– Evans, V., & Dooley, J. (2007). *Upstream intermediate*. Newbury Berkshire, UK: Express.
– Evans, V., & Edwards, L. (2008). *Upstream advanced*. Newbury Berkshire, UK: Express.

Analysis of the Profiles

After I had created the above profiles of my participants, I began a constant comparative reading of the profiles, looking for common themes that could inform my research and shed light on the current EFL teaching strategies in Poland, as well as personal characteristics. My role in the study was of an observer, without passing any judgment on the ways the participants instructed in order to develop their students' speaking, communicative, and cooperative skills. Below, the information is put into categories, in which I recognized commonalities, analyzed for emerging themes, and I drew conclusions drawn.

Five Common Themes of the Five Participants

Theme One: Participants' Experience with Grammatical/Grammar-Based Teaching

The Grammatical/Grammar-Based Approach, which is a teacher-centered approach, has been described as emphasizing a passive transfer of knowledge from teacher to student (Peyton et al., 2010). It has been used since the ancient times, when students were learning Latin and Greek until the middle of the 20th century (Brown, 2014). Today though the Grammatical/Grammar-Based Approach is considered to be an old-fashioned historical artifact (Canale, 1983; Cummins, 2001; Krashen, 1981; Ovando & Collier, 2011; Wong Fillmore & Valdez, 1986). However, the Grammatical/Grammar-Based Approach was the reality of communist Poland in the 1980s.

Four out of the five participants, all except Lidia, are in their middle and late forties; therefore, they were pre-high school age in the early and mid-1980s. Three out of the four participants (Anna, Barbara, and Maria) started learning the English language before they entered high school. What is interesting is that even though only one of the five participants, Lidia, is about 15 years on average younger than the rest of the participants, she too had still been exposed to the Grammatical/Grammar-Based Approach when she had attended private English classes, before she entered high school in the early 1990s. All the four participants who were exposed to the Grammatical/Grammar-Based English language approach shared very similar thoughts concerning their English learning experiences.

Anna recalls that during communism, learning a language was not connected to the world outside of the classroom. The lessons back then represented a traditional Grammatical/Grammar-Based Approach with drills, rote memorization, plenty of grammatical exercises, and almost no speaking of English in class by students. The English language learning process itself was quite monotonous, because that was what the communist educational system required; all teachers had to use the same textbooks, which were unappealing with almost no illustrations. The format of each lesson in the textbook looked the same; there was a reading, new vocabulary was explained through a direct translation from English to Polish, and students were required to do a few exercises concerning the readings. As researchers Barba (1997) and Mayer (1996) report, classes that frequently overused the text and lecture format resulted in student memorization of facts the students were to be tested on. Such facts are easily dropped from the students' long-term learning schemas and do little to build sustainable knowledge.

Barbara pointed out that the textbooks were very traditional, unappealing, and saturated with grammar and generic dialogs, but they were the only available resources in school back in the 1980s in Poland. The nature of dialogs in these texts that used the Grammatical/Grammar-Based Approach is discussed by Richards and Rogers (2001), who mention that drills and dialogs were designed to develop and enhance vocabulary and grammatical structures only. When language learners practiced these structures and dialogs, they would develop new structures, and it would become a habit. According to Barbara, there were also a lot of drills, repetitions, grammar teaching and grammar translation because, and she agreed, "A language teacher's job has been understood differently at different times and in different settings." Traditionally, the function of the teacher was to transmit knowledge, give instructions and control the process of student language learning (Wierbińska, 2009).

Helena did not experience learning English as a young child, but she has memories of experiencing the Grammatical/Grammar-Based Approach at the beginning of high school. She described this methodology then as a passive grammar translation methodology, with a lot of grammar and sentence translation from English to Polish or Polish to English, and sentence transformation where students had to change basic forms to a grammatically appropriate format in a given sentence. The teachers spoke Polish most of the time in class. It was dry teaching, as Helena called it. She agreed with Richards and Rogers (1986) describing the Grammatical/Grammar-Based Approach, who say "Instruction was typically conducted in the students' native language. This resulted in the type of grammar-translation courses remembered with distaste by thousands of school learners, for whom foreign language learning meant a tedious experience of memorizing endless lists of unusable grammar rules and vocabulary and attempting to produce perfect translations of stilted or literary prose (pp. 3–4).

Lidia stated than when she was learning English as a child, her English teacher was tough in a very traditional way. There was a lot of memorization of vocabulary and irregular verbs. There were drills and repetitions and no games at all. The teacher stressed pronunciation and even shouted at the students if there was something wrong about their pronunciation. The textbooks were very traditional, focusing mainly on grammar, and they had no pictures at all. A teacher was in the center of the classroom and the center of attention, and the learners were passively absorbing knowledge passed to them, absolutely dependent on their teachers. The traditional teacher's role was also to reinforce accurate language production in their students, and error correction was done through consistent feedback (Terrell et al., 1982).

Maria mentioned that as a child she attended private lessons given by a Catholic nun. The teaching was very grammar-translation based with a lot of grammatical exercises and almost no opportunities for students to speak English. The textbooks had almost no pictures, just grammatical exercises. There was no revision of vocabulary, and the teacher spoke Polish all the time to her students as well. Her private English lessons involved only six to eight students, but the teacher did not encourage dialog practice between them. This way of teaching is in accordance with the Grammatical/Grammar-Based Approach emphasizing that the student's native language is the medium of instruction (Richards & Rogers, 2014). It was a very traditional, passive, and old-fashioned way of learning twice a week in a group of eight students.

All the participants experienced the Grammatical/Grammar-Based Approach at the beginning of their English learning journeys, and saw it as lack of opportunities to speak English. The teaching-learning process was boring, passive, monotonous, and deprived of visualization and realia, focused on memorization and mechanical exercises taken from textbooks that were dull. Learning English did not relate to the reality outside of the classroom, and it was not connected with students' thoughts, opinions, feelings, and experiences.

Theme Two: Development of Students' Speaking, Communicative, and Cooperative Skills

Now as teachers, all five participants spoke English most of the time in their classes and expected their students to respond and interact in English as well in order to develop their speaking, communicative, and cooperative skills. All five participants, despite experiencing the Grammatical/Grammar-Based Approach when learning English were aware of the importance of the role and approach of communicative teaching and the development of speaking, communicative, and cooperative skills in their students. The five participants knew that learners used language for a purpose, therefore, the role of the teacher and the students was to provide a context for authentic communication, as memorizing patterns did not do much for the process of learning a language (Herrera & Murry, 2011). Instead, language development took place when students obtained comprehensive input, and when they interact in authentic, low-anxiety, risk-free, and language-abundant environments (Blair, 1982; Terrell, 1991). Lozanov (1982) adds that a relaxing, low anxiety and risk-free environment (created for example through playing music in the background) is of significant importance in learning a language and enhances language acquisition. So is the importance of the low affective filter. When students experience low anxiety and low stress levels, their affective filter is low, and they learn a language more effectively (Krashen as cited in Herrera & Murry, 2011). The Communicative Approach as pointed out by Spiteri (2010), "...emphasizes communication and speaking, meaningful input, contextualized grammar, and interactive activities through pair work and group work" (p. 131).

The five participants built their awareness of the importance of speaking and interaction in their classes through education, time, and exposure to communicative methodology experiences. All of the five participants utilized a variety of activities to promote the Communicative Approach in the ways they taught English. They used warm-up questions, speeches, dialogs, interviews, discussions, debates, picture descriptions and such. Therefore, students played active roles in their English language education. As the students learn a language, authentic and meaningful communication should be the goal of classroom activities (Richards & Rogers, 2014).

The five participants contributed to the fact that the students generated authentic discussions connecting lesson themes with their realities, interests, thoughts, opinions, emotions, and so forth. This is in line with DelliCarpini (2008) who says:

> When students are familiar with a topic, or are able to connect the topic to events or situations in their own lives, comprehension is increased and motivation enhanced. In order to engage secondary level ESL students, teachers must find commonalities between the text under investigation and the learners' lives. (p. 5)

The five participants gave up their teacher-centered roles and shifted to using student-centered teaching strategies, in which students spoke English, inter-acted, communicated, and cooperated with classmates. The five participants became more quiet and withdrawn observers while teaching, facilitating development of students' speaking skills, and their interactions. The concept of a withdrawn and quiet teacher is strongly encouraged by one of the most prolific educators of the 20th century, Caleb Gattegno (Gattegno, 1970).

Dewey (1897/2011), so revolutionary for his time in terms of education, observed a necessity of this type of teacher's role more than 100 years ago, and stated teacher should not be one to stand at the front of the room doling out bits of information to be absorbed by passive students. Instead of being in control of the students' educational process, the five participants shifted their roles to mediators, monitors, and scaffolders, who are not only knowledge-giv-ers, but learners as well. This concept is also discussed by Vygotsky (1934/1978), who emphasized the idea of the importance of interpersonal communication and social interaction with a skillful tutor in the process of learning. Menezes (2008) also highlights that based on Vygotskian thoughts, language learning is a socially mediated process.

All five participants saw a necessity to use various TPSI group configura-tions of students. A variety of the group configurations made the process of learning English more interesting, and students felt more comfortable inter-acting with each other rather than individually in front of the class. Brumfit (1984) claims, "We have seen that the use of pair and group work is the only available basis for naturalistic behavior in conversational interaction in class, and that work on this basis can increase the amount and intensity of practice during oral work" (p. 87). The five participants agreed with this statement, as through various group configuration activities, students were able to practice their speaking, communicative, and cooperative skills. They learned to be creative, flexible, patient, and tolerant with other team partners' ideas, skills so necessary in their future personal and professional life. Defined by Crystal (2003) as face-to-face communication with particular prosody, facial expres-sions, silence and rhythmical patterns of behavior, interactions between the participants is the key to the development of student's speaking, communica-tive, and cooperative skills.

Anna. Anna promoted speaking skills in her students by speaking about 95 percent of the time in English to her students, and they in return were expected to respond in the English language as well. She made her students speak not only on the lesson topic, but also to use English in their everyday situations. For instance, if something happened outside and students saw it out of the classroom window, Anna asked her students to express their ideas about it.

Anna offered her students various movies and videos on YouTube, where students had opportunities to discuss (usually in pairs first) and then to share with the whole class their observations, new vocabulary, and grammatical structures. She asked her students to create scenarios for role-play activities with a specific focus on the new vocabulary and grammatical structures recently learned. The role-plays gave students opportunities to work in small groups and in this way to develop their speaking, communicative, cooperative, and negotiating skills, possession of which is so useful in the world outside of the classroom. Then the role-plays were presented, recorded, and analyzed in an oral form by the students in terms of the content and form. Sometimes, Anna asked her students to prepare dialogs in pairs with the same follow-up procedure as in small group activities.

Anna included using idioms to make her students speak, communicate, and cooperate. For example, each student was asked to prepare a quote in English on a given topic and share the finding and thoughts on the quote with the whole class. Anna then connected the quotes with a real life situation and asked the students about the quote in connection with their personal lives. When moments of silence occurred, she prompted her students and turned the quote presentation into a whole class discussion by asking "Wh" questions. Anna made sure that each student contributed to the discussion, thus all the students had opportunities to practice their speaking skills in English. This activity also provided the students opportunities to share their personal thoughts and ideas, to identify the topic of the lesson with their lives outside of the classroom, to reflect on a given topic in connection with their personal lives, and to practice their speaking skills.

Another way of making students practice their speaking, communicative, and cooperative skills was working in pairs and creating dialogs, which students then needed to act out in front of the class. This created an authentic atmosphere through voice modulation, emotional expressions, decorations, costumes, and dramatizing, as students were supposed to use new vocabulary recently learned. The students were also strongly encouraged to speak and improvise when necessary and they were discouraged to read scripts for the dialogs. Even though the students prepared the exercises with their elbow or pair partners, the teacher often chose two random students to improvise the dialog and to practice for the final oral exam, as during the exam the students would have to improvise with an examiner. During the pair configuration activity, students were provided with an opportunity to practice their speaking, communicative, cooperative, and improvisational skills, and prepare a successful, authentic sounding dialog. Through the dialogs, the students were able to review the new vocabulary and consolidated it.

Anna used debates to make students speak, communicate, and cooperate in English. She prepared controversial topics with two opposite opinions that could be expressed as pros and cons of a situation. Students needed to decide which view they supported, then they had to communicate and cooperate with the rest of the group to produce arguments supporting their statements. Anna monitored the debates, as sometimes they could turn into heated discussions. She valued her students' opinions, as long as they presented coherent, logical, and convincing arguments.

During almost every class, Anna prepared a short visual activity for her students as a practice for their oral final exam. For example, she presented a picture to describe asking, "Where/who/what was/were/she/he/they doing in a given picture?" The students were also able to relate to the picture, talking about their own lives in association with the theme of the picture. During the activity, students were able to practice their speaking skills and identify with the topic.

Sometimes Anna asked her students to prepare pictures in hard copy or use a cellphone or tablet to present. The students needed to share ideas and opinions about them, answering the question of why they selected a particular picture. Through the activity, students were able to practice their speaking skills and broaden their general content area knowledge on the given picture and topic it concerned. Often a picture presentation changed into discussions, during which students not only practiced their speaking skills, but communicative skills as well.

Barbara. Barbara used English all the time in class to motivate students to speak English, and her students were strongly encouraged to respond in English as well. The Polish language was used only if absolutely necessary to explain and understand the English vocabulary that could not be understood by students. She introduced speeches, drama, role-play, and made the students create scenarios on various topics associated with class themes. When students were asked to prepare speeches on a given topic, Barbara made all the students be active while one student presented a speech, as the rest of the students sat in chairs in a horseshoe shape and they had to prepare questions for the presenter. The above activities contributed to the development of students' brainstorming, speaking, communicative, and cooperative skills, and students learned to express their ideas and emotions using the English language.

Barbara often used elbow/pair partner work when students focused on the creation of meaningful dialogs, either to practice new vocabulary, new grammatical structures, or both. Students practiced dialogs in pairs and then Barbara selected a few pairs, or sometimes even different students in a pair, to create improvised dialogs. The students not only had opportunities to practice new material in the form of new vocabulary and/or new grammatical structures but they learned to be creative, innovative, flexible, and to improvise as they practiced their speaking, communicative, and cooperative skills. Students were often asked to describe pictures in pairs. Therefore, when talking to each other they could practice their speaking, communicative, and cooperative skills, and they could speculate on what was going on in a given picture.

Barbara used various TPSI group configurations. She said the variation was crucial to avoid boredom, but also to make sure that students communicated and cooperated with one another. Additionally, it provided an opportunity for students to be in a configuration that the students liked. Barbara observed that extroverts preferred pair and small group work, and introverts preferred to be in a total group or work individually. The various group configurations helped to build integration and interaction in a given class.

Whenever possible, Barbara attempted to connect lesson topics to reality. For instance, she connected the lesson themes to students' lives, asking them questions concerning their interests, hobbies, and everyday real situations. In this way, students practiced their English skills, and they were able to express their thoughts and opinions, had the feeling that their opinions mattered, and to take the lesson beyond the confinement of the four classroom walls.

In order to practice students' debating skills, Barbara often either provided a topic presenting two sides or two arguments, or she showed two pictures to her students, one presenting one argument and the other presenting an opposite argument. The students then chose a side of the classroom depending on which side they supported. Next, the class was divided into two groups. One group was asked to prepare arguments supporting its view, and the other group supported the opposite arguments. The groups worked with posters, and the debates were monitored by Barbara. The activity provided an opportunity for students to practice their logical thinking, speaking, argumentative, communicative, and cooperative skills.

Barbara also read stories and used skit creation to develop her students' interactive skills. Before a story was read, she only provided the title and made student think what the story might have been about. Then she read the story without the ending and asked the students to guess what the ending might have been. Through these activities, Barbara made her students brainstorm, speculate, and use their imagination when practicing their speaking skills.

Then in groups of three or four the students would act the story out. They prepared some decorations, divided their roles, and improvised the story. The students were able to organize themselves into groups of their own choice, which gave them a feeling of autonomy and ownership in their own learning. Through the activity, the students were able to practice their speaking, communicative, and cooperative skills. They learned to be creative, flexible, patient, and tolerant to other team partners' ideas, skills so necessary in their future personal and professional life.

Helena. Helena used English as the language of instruction most of the time and made her students speak English in class as well, except for clarifications. When the students used Polish, they were redirected by Helena to speak English. Helena carefully selected students to answer verbally, providing opportunities to all students to speak English during classes.

Helena worked on developing her students' speaking, communicative, and cooperative skills by using discussions, debates, open-ended questions, creation of dialogs with new vocabulary, and picture descriptions, including students' opinions and projects in class where students needed to negotiate. She often used brainstorming before any activity, verbal predictions of the new class topic, and pair or small group discussions.

One of the final exam requirements was to describe a picture. Therefore, Helena provided pictures for her students to describe individually. She often connected the activity with the use of newly learned vocabulary from previous lessons on given topics. This activity enabled Helena's students to practice new vocabulary concerning previous lessons and to use their speaking skills. Through practicing their imaginative and speculative skills, the students were able to express their personal ideas, opinions, and thoughts.

In discussions, Helena prompted her students to speak by asking them open-ended questions on a given topic. Sometimes she divided students into pairs for discussions, where they described pictures and images. Then, Helena asked some pairs to share the arguments they came up with when they describe them. Students also expressed their thoughts and opinions associated with the lesson topic and connected them to their life experiences. The activities also provided them opportunities to practice their speaking, communicative, argumentative, and cooperative skills while working with their pair partners.

Another activity Helena used to practice her students' verbal skills was a chain story activity. The students read a story and then they had to retell the story in their own words, including students' input, such as opinions, ideas, and thoughts. Therefore, each of them was supposed to produce one sentence until the story was fully told. Therefore, each student has an equal chance to verbally participate in the speaking activity. The students were required to use sequencing vocabulary, e.g., at first, at the beginning, then, next, finally, at last and such. This activity provided students opportunities to practice their speaking, communicative, and cooperative skills. They also were able to learn new vocabulary; practice sequencing vocabulary; share their own personal stories, feelings, and emotions; and identify the content of the class in connection with real life situations.

Debate was another activity Helena used to develop her students' verbal skills. Identifying the pros and cons of arguments, and debating the advantages and disadvantages of particular subjects were frequent in Helena's style of teaching. The students needed to think about what side they supported. The students who saw the pros/advantages of a given situation sat on the right side of the classroom, and the students who saw the cons/disadvantages sat on the left side of the classroom. This activity provided students opportunities to practice for the final exams, since during the actual exam they would receive a topic to develop. The students were also able to practice their brainstorming, logical thinking, speaking, communicative, cooperative, debating, and argumentative skills, and connect their thoughts and ideas to real world situations.

Lidia. Lidia spoke English almost all the time in class, and the students who responded in Polish were redirected to speak English to encourage the development of their speaking skills. Only on special occasions to avoid misunderstandings was the Polish language used in her classes.

In order to develop students' speaking skills, Lidia used warm-up questions and activities, speeches, discussions, debates, skits, dialogs, and conversations with her students. This gave students opportunities to practice vocabulary from a given area, agree or disagree, and to express their opinions, feelings, and emotions.

Lidia was aware of the importance of the final exam. Therefore, she utilized activities often used during the exam, such as warm-up questions, picture descriptions, and discussions on the advantages and disadvantages of some situations, which taught students logical thinking, and raised questions concerning their experience. For the purpose of practice for the final oral exam, Lidia frequently began lessons by presenting a picture to her students. The students needed to describe the picture in pairs and to connect it with their own personal feelings and emotions. Lidia prompted her students by starting with "Wh" open-ended questions. Through the activities, students were able to practice their speaking, communicative, and cooperative skills, and connect with their own realities.

Lidia tried to prepare her students not only to be fluent in English, but also to think and speak maturely, because the pictures the students were asked to describe and reflect on were challenging, even if the students had to describe them in Polish. Lidia conducted mock oral final exams of English. She took questions from previous years and practiced them with a student one exam set at a time, so the students had a feeling of the one-on-one exam and they were better emotionally and mentally prepared.

Speeches were also popular in Lidia's classes, but with older students who were more proficient in English and had better skills to produce coherent speeches. According to Lidia, her students needed to be mature to deliver speeches. Lidia was also an enthusiast of projects, role-plays, skits, and theater, because through these activities, students were entertained, and they improved their English skills without even realizing it. Lidia also did mini-projects with her students where they needed to brainstorm ideas, speak to each other, communicate, and cooperate.

Creation of dialogs by students was a common way of developing students' speaking and interactive skills. Usually divided into pairs, students were asked to create dialogs associated with the theme of a lesson, but the dialogs needed to be authentic and connected with the world surrounding the students. The dialogs often led to whole class discussions. During such activities, Lidia's students were able to practice their speaking, communicative, cooperative, argumentative, and interactive skills in an authentic language learning environment that reached outside of the four classroom walls. They were also able to express their thoughts, ideas, and opinions.

Debates were common activities Lidia used to promote the development of speaking skills in English, where students who agreed with a lesson point were on one side of the room and these who disagreed were on the other side. Lidia monitored the debates, making sure each side provided arguments which supported the statement. Lidia made sure that each student contributed verbally to a debate. Debate activities enabled the students to practice their logical thinking, speaking, communicative, cooperative, argumentative, interactive, and debating skills. The students were also able to connect the class topic to their own realities.

As far as group configurations were concerned, Lidia used pair work more often than small groups. Students liked working in pairs because they felt less stressed and intimidated than when talking in front of the whole class. In small groups, it was often one student that was a leader and took over the group, and the rest of the students might not have necessarily been working together. Therefore, it was important that Lidia walked around the classroom and checked the groups' progress. Lidia felt pair work was crucial, as students needed to work on their speaking, communicative, and cooperative skills.

Maria. Maria spoke English most of the time in her classes to promote the development of students' speaking skills. If students responded in Polish, she redirected them to English as the native tongue of the students was used rarely, only in emergency situations when the students had absolutely no understanding of a given notion, vocabulary, or a grammatical nuance.

Maria claimed that developing speaking skills was crucial in her teaching philosophy. She explained from the very beginning to her students that they would have to speak and talk a lot in her classes. Students were motivated to prepare speeches, presentations, dialogs, interviews, debates, and verbal picture descriptions.

Maria asked her students to think, brainstorm, and research about the topic at home. The students were then asked to prepare speeches on world topics, connecting their research information, their opinions, and the topic to the reality of their lives. Maria made sure her students truly presented their speeches in front of the whole class instead of reading from a piece of paper. When it came to new vocabulary the class might hear, the presenting students were responsible for preparing the new words and phrases on the whiteboard, and then they were asked about their meaning in English first. If any of the new vocabulary was unknown to any of the students, the presenting students were responsible for explaining the unknown vocabulary through the use of synonyms, antonyms, and/or definitions in English.

This activity provided Maria's students with opportunities to speak English in class, become informed on world issues, reflect, question, and discuss the presented topics in connection with the reality of the contemporary world. The students also had opportunities to practice vocabulary from previous lessons and to learn new vocabulary. They were able to practice and develop their English skills in an environment resembling an authentic environment of the English world.

After the speeches, frequently whole class discussions developed, monitored by Maria, who asked additional questions to make students think and speak in English. The speech and discussion activities encouraged students to practice their speaking skills (especially public speaking skills), to learn new vocabulary, to reflect on the natural environment they lived in, and to express their thoughts, opinions, and concerns about the topic. Maria stressed the use of words associated with expressing opinions such as: I believe, in my opinion, I feel, I think, it seems to me that, to me, and such. This activity provided the students opportunities to practice for the final exams, as during the actual exam they would receive a topic to develop. The students also practiced their speaking, debating, and argumentative skills, and connected their thoughts and ideas to the real world.

Maria used dialogs to promote her students' speaking and interactive skills. When students were supposed to present dialogs in pairs, Maria selected three sets of pairs to present their work in front of the whole class. The students were not allowed to read their dialogs, only to present, to make the situation more natural and authentic. They practiced public speaking, a useful skill for the future.

The dialog pair activity provided the students with opportunities to practice their communicative and cooperative skills; to prepare a successful, authentic sounding dialog; and to practice their speaking skills. Through the dialogs the students were also able to review the new vocabulary and consolidate it.

One of the dialog forms Maria promoted in her classes was an interview, during which students needed to prepare new vocabulary and share them with the rest of the students. Maria made sure every student had an opportunity to say something in class and that newly learned vocabulary was utilized. Sometimes she selected volunteers to answer questions, but often she selected students to speak and answer questions. Otherwise, some students would never be active and speak in class.

Students often worked in teams of two, three, or four when there was a debate, usually in the form of pros and cons of a topic or an argument. Then they had to "sell" their knowledge to the rest of the class. Before any activity, brainstorming was important for students to think about a given topic. Maria found it challenging when working in teams, groups, or pairs, as students often switched to speaking Polish. However, many students used the opportunity to practice speaking English as much as possible.

In connection with the final exam requirement, Maria presented pictures to her students in order for them to describe, to express their opinions verbally, and to associate them with the surrounding world. Maria used hard copy images, photographs, images from the Internet, and pictures from the textbooks, which were often connected with exemplary exercises for the final exams. The images were always associated with the topic of a given lesson, which gave Maria's students opportunities to practice vocabulary concerning a given lesson or unit theme. This activity provided opportunities to the students to practice their speaking skills using newly acquired vocabulary from previous lessons and to practice a picture description skill for their final oral exam. If picture description was done in pairs, then students additionally practiced their communicative and cooperative skills as well.

Maria realized various TPSI group configurations were important in the process of teaching and learning, thus students were kept interested, and they could develop their speaking, communicative, and cooperative skills. Students worked for instance in pairs when they described pictures and created dialogs and interviews. Students were arranged in small groups of three to four when they worked on projects with posters, brainstormed ideas, and created final products. They also worked in small groups when they wrote summaries together, bulleted ideas, discussed pros and cons of topics, and so forth. The use of small groups was something that changed in Maria's way of teaching, as previously it was more individualized where students worked on their own.

Theme Three: The Use of Technology in the Classroom

Youth have a strong interest in technology, and technology continues to be popular in teaching and learning (Blair, 2012). Incorporation of technological tools such as computers, audio and video cameras, software, and an overhead projector makes the teaching and learning experience more interesting, powerful, and richer. Research demonstrates that the use of technology motivates EFL and ESL learners (Traore & Kyei-Blankson, 2011), and also acts as "a stimulus for language development" (Butler-Pascoe & Wiburg, 2003, p. 84). Through the use of technology, teachers have an ability to create student-friendly, non-threatening environments and safe spaces, where students can feel free to take risks and engage in new learning, so they can develop their critical thinking abilities and share their ideas and thoughts.

Computers combine voice, image, color, and motion, activating students' senses, which helps to enhance their language skills. For example, they can visually remember new vocabulary, pronunciation of new words, etc. Butler-Pascoe and Wiburg (2003) state, "Computers allow teachers to add multisensory elements, text, sound, picture, video, and animation, which provide meaningful contexts to facilitate comprehension" (p. 84). Computers are also of a nonjudgmental nature, providing students with the ability to review material numerous times without being exposed to embarrassment, fear, or anxiety, and they can change the new learning into comprehensive input (Butler-Pascoe & Wiburg, 2003).

Computers also promote communication and cooperation among EFL and ESL students if they are assigned to perform a group activity. As Bowman and Plaisir (1996) say, "Teamwork is essential to the success of the projects and students realize that they must work together if they are to complete the activities" (p. 27). Freire (2000) mentions, "I've no doubt about the enormous potential for technology to motivate and challenge children and adolescents…" (p. 82).

The five participants believed that technology could aid in teaching too, especially now when new generations of students are practically brought up on computers, tablets, and smart phones. In the five participants' opinions, the Internet and various computer programs were not only endless sources of information for students and helpful methodological aids, but they also were a means of communication between educators and students. It is definitely easier and more motivating to learn when we like something.

Therefore, all five participants included the use of technology with their students. Each classroom was equipped with an overhead projector and a teacher's computer. The five participants also had access to the Internet and they used images, pictures, and visuals for students to work on, as well as online dictionaries, and PowerPoint presentations prepared by themselves and their students. The five participants used available online movies, and documentaries, or clips to broaden students' vocabulary in English. They also used YouTube videos for various purposes, such as teaching new vocabulary (e.g., through songs), grammar, cultural aspects about English-speaking countries, and so forth. In order for their students to understand more about the daily news of English-speaking countries, each of the five participants utilized news programs or clips from the BBC, CNN, the Discovery Channel, and such.

Three out of the five of the participants have access to an interactive board in their classrooms. The textbooks of these three participants were compatible with the interactive board. Therefore, students could do exercises on the board by moving parts of words or sentences with their fingers.

All five participants used CDs and DVDs in their classes as well. They were usually materials attached to textbooks, their private collections, are owned by the school or public libraries. They had similar functions as the Internet sources.

Theme Four: Student-Centered Instruction in EFL Classroom

The five participants put effort into making an environment in which their students felt the teaching and learning process was centered around them, instead of a situation, where the teacher was not the one who stood at the front of the room doling out bits of information out to be absorbed by passive students (Dewey, 1897/2011). Instead of being in control of the students' educational process, the five participants shifted their roles to mediators, monitors, and scaffolders who were not only knowledge-givers but learners as well, as mentioned by Vygotsky (1934/1978), who emphasized the idea of interpersonal communication and social interaction with a skillful tutor in the process of learning. Dewey (1916/1963) also mentions that students learn more by doing and experiencing than by observing only. That skillful tutor can be the teacher, another more knowledgeable student helping other student/students, or even the teacher learning from their students. This kind of interpersonal and social interaction was observed during interactive activities introduced by the five participants in their instruction.

It was observed that each of the five participants scaffolded their teaching to their students. As Herrera and Murry (2011) put it, instruction can be scaffolded through hands-on activities, social interaction, cooperative learning, and visual support, such as images, objects, manipulatives, and realia. For example, when students described pictures individually or in pairs, the five participants prompted the students with questions that made students think and provide answers corresponding to the prompts.

The five participants had their students play active roles in their English language education through various interactive activities, such as warm-up questions, speeches, dialogs, interviews, discussions, debates, picture description, games, songs, exercises, and such, performed by students individually, in pairs, or in groups. "Through participation in these interactive activities, students are engaged in what they are studying" (Brown, 2008, p. 30). For example, in discussions and debates, the five participants asked questions and led students to solutions, as recommended by Brooks and Brooks (2000), who advise asking questions and directing students to solutions rather than just providing answers. Keeping the goal in mind of feeding student's natural curiosity, Brown (2008) recommends that "…the teacher becomes a coach, or instigator, who is always there to assist, but never to give away answers" (p. 33).

During pair work, group work, and dialog creation, students experience interpersonal communication and social interaction (Vygotsky, 1934/1978). In the activities where the students either interact with each other or with their teachers, they experience a socially mediated process, a Vygotskian concept highlighted by Menezes (2008). Students can also practice their leadership and shared leadership skills.

The interactive activities mentioned above allowed the students of the five participants to think, brainstorm, and connect the topic of the lesson to their personal experiences, realities, identities, and opinions. The students felt free to agree or disagree, as long as they provided coherent arguments supporting their statements. The students also felt safe and the low anxiety environment created by the five participants allowed the students to express their personal emotions and feelings in connection to the class topics. The five participants create a friendly classroom environment which was in accordance with Lozanov (1982), who says that relaxing, low anxiety and risk-free environment is of significant importance in learning a language, which can enhance language acquisition. Krashen, cited in Herrera and Murry (2011) also talks about the importance of student friendly environment in the process of learning a language.

When the environment is low-stress and friendly in discussing and debating activities the five participants' students had opportunities to practice and develop their brainstorming, reflective, logical thinking, debating, and argumentative skills. In dialog activities the students were able to practice their creative, improvising, innovative, and inventive skills.

The five participants realized that teaching the English language was not a goal itself anymore; it was a means through which students learned numerous skills, skills necessary to successfully function in society and in students' personal and professional lives after they graduated from high school. Through this type of teaching students "...become self-sufficient, creative thinkers and achieve independent minds" (Brown, 2008, pp. 33–34).

By keeping students at the center of the classroom, the five participants "... encourage and inspire students to seek out knowledge and to strive for understanding at a deeper level" (Brown, 2008, p. 35). Through interactive activities, the five participants provided opportunities for their students to participate in their own process of learning, connected to lessons to their lives, realities, and contemporary life outside of the classroom. Students had voices and felt that their voices counted when they connected the class topics to their interests and their hobbies, their customs and traditions, their religion and culture. Students saw the meaning and the purpose of their learning. As mentioned by Crowell et al. (1998), "Learning becomes personal when we allow it to have meaning for individual students and when we relate that meaning to a sense of purpose and connectedness" (p. 51). In this way, when students make connections between class topics, their realities, and the world outside of the classroom, they are involved in the meaning-making process and ultimately are learning more willingly, effectively, and efficiently. As mentioned by McCombs and Whisler (1997), learning is most meaningful when topics and class themes can be applied to students' interests, educational needs, and lives in general. CALLA (Cognitive Academic Language Learning Approach), the previously mentioned teaching method, also emphasizes in the teaching-learning process the importance of such components as: valuing students' prior knowledge and cultural experiences, and relating this knowledge to academic learning and developing language awareness (Herrera & Murry, 2011).

In the case of the five participants and their students, student-centered instruction was also possible thanks to such factors like pair and small group work. The fact that there were only about 15 students in each group, which meant the five participants were more effectively able to promote interactive activities in their classes and a more individualized teaching style.

What is interesting, none of the five participants were familiar with the term CALLA. However, all of the student-centered principles of CALLA were present in their classrooms; scaffolding; valuing students' prior knowledge and cultural experiences; relating this knowledge to academic learning in a new language and culture; social interaction; successful working with others; learning through cooperative learning tasks; and how to become more effective and independent learners (Herrera & Murry, 2011).

Theme Five: Teaching and Learning in an Authentic Environment
The five participants faced a challenging situation in making the English language process meaningful and authentic to their EFL students, as they

lived in an environment where all the students were Polish and their native language was Polish. Selinger (1988) says that EFL and ESL students "...have little or no exposure to the second language outside the classroom" (p. 27). Brown (2014) declares that "Few if any people achieve fluency in a foreign language solely within the confines of the classroom" (p. 1). This sounds quite pessimistic, however, the situation did not look so negative in the case of these five participating teachers. They all put effort towards making the learning of English authentic to their students by focusing on the following five aspects of authentic English teaching and learning: classroom decorations, connecting with students' reality, using songs and games, using authentic materials, and taking students on trips to workshops and language camps where they used English to communicate.

Classroom Decorations. All five participants decorated their classrooms with materials that created an authentic and motivating environment for students to learn the English language. The materials included maps, images, posters, pictures of the United Kingdom, and the United States, and photos of students traveling to different countries for trips and workshops, where they used English as the means of communication.

Connecting with Students' Realities. Learners need to make connections between the language and content they are learning in class and their own realities in the world (Coatney, 2006). The topics that interest students include family, raising children, communicating effectively, and such (Weinstein, 1999). Therefore, the five participants connected their students' experiences, interests, prior knowledge, opinions, feelings, and emotions, through speeches and interactive activities, such as pair work, group projects, and so forth. This happened, for example, when students talked about their families, did job interviews, participated in virtual trips, and debated on topics that were in the news on a given day.

Using Song and Games. Activities such as games and songs provide students with joy, fun, and learning through laughter and healthy competition, and they are a natural and authentic way of learning a language. Klancar (2006) states, "Using songs, poems, rhymes and chants is a wonderful way of making students sing/talk and at the same time (unconsciously) work at their grammar, vocabulary, and pronunciation" (para. 2). All of the five participants shared this opinion, and therefore, they taught their students English using Christmas carols, national songs, and songs popular in a given year to reach their students through their love of music and musical interests. Students could then connect and identify their English language learning process with the songs they liked. The five participants also were fond of games such as *Hangman* and *Shark.*

Using Authentic Materials. One of the ways to create a more authentic class-room environment is using authentic materials in English classes. Jordan (1997) refers to authentic texts as "...texts that are not written for language teaching purposes (p. 113). As discussed by Guariento and Morley (2001), "Authentic materials are significant since they increase students' motivation for learning, makes the learner be exposed to the 'real' language" (p. 347). The main advantages of using authentic materials are that they provide real cultural information, access to the native English language, and a positive effect on students' motivation, plus they are more associated with students ' needs and support a more creative approach to teaching and learning (Philips & Shettlesworth, 1978; Clarke, 1989; Peacock, 1997, as cited in Richards, 2001).

The use of authentic materials in the classroom is exciting for both teachers and students. Chavez (1998) mentions that learners enjoy dealing with authentic materials as they enable learners to interact with the real language and its use. Therefore, all five participants used authentic materials in their classes, including magazine and newspaper articles, online articles meant for native speakers of English, British publications, tests for students published in the United Kingdom, movies, online videos, and newscasts targeted at the English as a first language population. The five participants realized that it was crucial that students interacted with the native English language outside of the classroom, and that interaction created and increased students' interest and motivation towards the English language.

Students on Trips, Workshops, and Language Camps. In order for students to have a deeper authentic experience of learning English, it is crucial that at some point in their English education, students are exposed to the use of English in a natural environment, which means either spending time in a country where the native language is English, such as the United Kingdom, or going to another country where students will be able to communicate in English. As suggested by Tseng (2002), culture effects and changes an individual's perception and is vital for expanding an individual's perspective of the world. According to Stuart and Nocon (1996), "Learning about the lived culture of actual target language speakers as well as about one's own culture requires tools that assist language learners in negotiating meaning and understanding the communicative and cultural texts in which linguistic codes are used" (p. 432).

For that purpose, all five participants either organized trips for students, such as language camps, or participated in workshops with students in the United Kingdom and other countries, where students could communicate in a natural English language environment. For instance, they did this by listening to a guide in a museum; ordering a meal in a restaurant; conversing with host families they stayed with; or buying a ticket or a soda. In other words, students were exposed to the living language and they felt the need to speak and use their English language skills (Shanahan, 1997).

Summary

In this chapter, I presented the five participating teachers through their interviews and class observations. I also revealed the findings of the five commonalities I found between the participants when comparing their stories from interviews and class observations. The five commonalties were: the participants' experience with Grammatical/Grammar-Based Approach; the development of students' speaking, communicative, and cooperative skills; the use of technology in the classroom; student-centered instruction in the EFL classroom; and teaching and learning in an authentic environment.

In Chapter 5, I discuss what all the commonalities meant and talked about other aspects of the study, such as the methodology revision I used. I also remind my readers about the context of the study, summarize the findings from Chapter 4, discuss the limitations of the study, provide suggestions for future research, and reflect on my journey as a researcher.

Discussion

Introduction

This qualitative case study was guided by my curiosity regarding the ways teachers taught English as a Foreign Language in public schools in Poland. I gathered qualitative data through data collection instruments, such as class observations and interviews (Creswell, 2007; Eisenhard, 1989), to learn about five participating teachers' paths to becoming EFL teachers, their transformations through political and educational changes, and the ways the teachers today manifest their pedagogical practices in order to develop their students' speaking, communicative, and cooperative skills in the English language.

Review of Methodology

I chose a qualitative research paradigm and case study as a "qualitative approach to inquiry" (Creswell, 2007, p. 53) to collect my research data, which enabled me to understand and interpret the experiences and social interactions of five participants as students of EFL, becoming EFL public high school teachers, and with their students during their journeys in obtaining their EFL education.

As mentioned previously, the instrumentation used in this study was class observations and interviews with the five participating teachers. I chose observations as they provided a systematic description of events (Marshall & Rossman, 1989) and a written photograph of the situation under study (Erlandson et al., 1993). I also interviewed each of the five participating public high school teachers, which were described as social events that needed to be nurtured, sustained, and gracefully ended (Dexter, 2006; Hayman et al., 1954; Mishler, 1986).

In order to obtain data for this study, I moved to southern Poland for three months to conduct classroom observations and interviews. The observations took place in the school where the five participants worked as EFL teachers. Between February and May, 2015, I attended the participants' classes and observed them in their natural environment. I witnessed their lived experiences.

The five participants were also interviewed in places and the language of their preference: native Polish or English. They all chose to be interviewed in

© KONINKLIJKE BRILL NV, LEIDEN, 2019 | DOI:10.1163/9789004394377_005

Polish, and the following topic was addressed along with the following questions. I explained to the teachers the purpose of my dissertation research, which I shared as follows:

> This is a qualitative case study of five English as a Foreign Language (EFL) public high school teachers in Poland, their stories of learning English, and the ways they manifest their pedagogical practices to develop and enhance their students' speaking, communicative, and cooperative skills in the English language.

The overarching question for my research was: How do five EFL teachers in Poland manifest their pedagogical practices? This general research question contained several sub-questions.

> *Sub-question 1*) What kinds of experience and educational preparation do the five Polish EFL teachers have?
> *Sub-question 2*) How do Polish EFL teachers describe their EFL methodologies as related to their students' speaking, communicative, and cooperative skills, and how is their philosophy manifested in a classroom setting?
> *Sub-question 3a*) How do these EFL teachers reflect on teaching practices prior to and subsequent to the fall of communism?
> *Sub-question 3b*) Given that there are social, economic, and pedagogical differences in EFL pre- and post-communism, what evidence do the teachers provide that their practices in teaching EFL have changed over time?

In the *first part* of the interview, which I called *historical*, the five participants recounted their past experiences as students and teachers of English. In the *second part* of the interview, which I called *contemporary*, the participants were asked to describe how they taught to promote the speaking, communicative, and cooperative skills of their students. In the *third part* of the interview, which I called *reflective* (while keeping in mind the answers to the participants' first two questions), they were asked to reflect on their teaching practices in association with developing their students' speaking, communicative, and cooperative skills.

The data received from the five participating teachers was transcribed and translated from Polish into English. Profiles of the five participants were created containing direct quotations from the participants. The data then were analyzed, compared, synthesized, and conclusions were drawn.

The findings of this research will be shared with other members in the EFL field so they will be able to take into consideration and incorporate my study, and in this way enhance and enrich their teaching-learning methodology in their institutions and communities. This research will also be informative to instructors in countries where English is spoken as a native language. The findings in my research that these instructors may find useful is what Polish EFL teachers do or do not do in terms of enhancing their foreign learners' English speaking, communicative, and cooperative skills. These instructors will learn from my study and will be able to incorporate the knowledge into their own teaching practices. The findings from this research will be made public, thus EFL teachers, curriculum designers, and policy makers not only in Poland but also in other non-native English speaking countries and native English-speaking countries can benefit from the findings in designing their curricula.

Contextualization of the Research

Poland has gone through significant political, social, cultural, economic, and educational changes in the last few decades. In the 1960s, English was introduced as a mandated subject in Polish public high schools (Reichelt, 2005). The instruction of English was boring, disconnected from reality, and teachers used uninteresting and unappealing textbooks (Ehrenhalt, 1990). After school, students were able to attend English courses offered by different educational and cultural institutions. However, the quality of instruction was as bad as in high school (Ehrenhalt, 1990).

In the 1970s, the popularity of English continued to grow in Poland (Muchisky, 1985), and by the 1980s, studying English became the most studied foreign language in the country (British Council, 1986). In the 1990s, Poles became more motivated to study English, as they started seeing their knowledge of English could help them in their future careers and economic status (Varney, 1984).

The fall of communism in Poland in 1989 (Odrowaz, 2009) and shifting the teaching of English towards a Communicative Approach in Western countries put the English teachers in Poland in a situation in which they had to explore new teaching methodologies, establish new courses, and find teaching materials suitable to the new educational, social, cultural, political, and economic situations in Poland.

During the intervening years since communism, times and culture have changed; Poland is not behind the "Iron Curtain" anymore. The country's borders opened. Poland has gone through a major transition process, in which the challenges for education in terms of new approaches to learning and teaching have been accompanied by vast social and political changes, such as the democratization of structures and processes (Dąbrowski & Wiśniewski, 2011).

Since the early 1990s, the Polish education and training system has undergone a complex series of reforms. Several of these changes in the Polish educational system occurred simultaneously, and significant shifts in the learning and teaching process were brought about by numerous international influences. The process of learning and teaching EFL in Poland became influenced, in particular, by various student-centered, cooperative, and communicative teaching approaches. There is urgency among teachers of EFL to find creative ways to enhance their EFL students' abilities to learn English as close to the fluency of native speakers as possible.

Each of the five participants in this study lived through the cultural, socioeconomic, political, and educational challenges and changes in Poland, which shaped their teaching EFL philosophies and methodologies. Their methodology was revised through time and through gaining life and teaching experiences.

Summary of Findings

The five participants share numerous similarities and commonalities in their lived experiences, teaching philosophies, and teaching methods. The following five commonalities were found between them:

- All five participants were exposed to the Grammatical/Grammar-Based Approach to teaching and learning English as young learners.
- All the participants shifted to a teaching approach focusing on the development of speaking, communicative, and cooperative skills in students learning the English language.
- Technology was present and used in each of the five participants' EFL instruction.
- There was a strong presence of student-centered teaching philosophy in all five participants' classrooms.
- All five participants expressed a preference for authentic teaching-learning processes.

Commonality One: Participants' Experience with Grammatical/ Grammar-Based Approach

Poland used the Grammatical/Grammar-Based Approach and all five participants experienced this approach and its methodology either in the classroom when learning English, or during their education through private lessons. During their early English education, they experienced boring English classes, unappealing textbooks, no group or pair work, and no connection between the content English knowledge and the five participants' realities, hobbies, interests, or experiences. There was no interaction and hardly any speaking of English during the lessons. The five participants remembered learning a lot of grammar and memorizing lists of English vocabulary. Their learning of English was very passive.

At that time the participants did not realize there was anything wrong or inappropriate with that type of teaching and learning, as it was the reality of learning English in Poland during communist times. A passive transfer of knowledge from teacher to student (Peyton et al., 2010) was considered as a normalcy without even being able to realize alternatives.

However, this type of learning had a huge impact on the five participants' development of English skills, as they were stressed and intimidated while learning English and unable to use their knowledge in the verbal form. There-fore, when they started learning English in high school, they all struggled to speak English in public; they were shy to do so and found it very stressful. They also did not experience critical thinking, connecting the class material with to realities, learning through realia and images, working in groups, and cooperat-ing with elbow and pair partners.

Commonality Two: Shift towards Speaking, Communicative, and Cooperative Skills

The political, educational, and technological changes that took place in Poland in the 1990's, such as the fall of communism, which led to the open-ing of borders, educational reform, and accessibility of computers and the Internet in Polish schools, had a huge impact on the five participants and the way they evolved to be the types of teachers of English they are today. All five participants underwent a process of awakening, discovery, and transfor-mation. They became more exposed to and familiar with teaching English literature, which promoted interactive and cooperative ways of teaching and learning English by internationally recognized linguists specializing in teach-ing English as a Second Language, including Dr. Steven Krashen and Dr. James Cummins.

However, the five participants needed to adjust their ESL knowledge gained from the ESL specialists to the conditions of the EFL classroom and their field, which was deprived of the everyday native English speaking environment. Since English is not spoken on an everyday basis in Poland, students relatively rarely experience the true authenticity of the English language. The five participants also gained access to new textbooks, which were colorful, with numerous pictures and more meaningful activities for students learning English.

The five participants started having "aha moments" when they realized that teaching and learning English according the rules of the Grammatical/

Grammar-Based Approach was not the way to go. They started challenging the Grammatical/Grammar-Based Approach. As Tobias (1992) says, "New thinking begins with a critique of old thinking" (p. 13). The five participants gained new ways of thinking, pointed out by Senge, as cited by Caine and Caine (1997b), "Nothing will change in the future without fundamentally new ways of thinking" (p. 14).

The five participants started experimenting and seeing how they could do activities differently with their students. The students became more interested in class topics. The participants noticed for instance, that if activities involved various group configurations, students became more involved in their own process of freely speaking, interacting, exchanging ideas, and creating projects together with their peers in the English language. These are skills that students can take with them to the professional world after they graduate from high school, college, or university, so they can be flexible successful future leaders, team players, empathetic and understanding supervisors, and employees. The five participants underwent a process of personal revelation and metamorphosis in terms of their philosophy of teaching English language.

Commonality Three: Presence of Technology in Teaching

Present generations of students grew up on computers, access to the Internet, and other technological devices (Blair, 2012). Research demonstrates English learners are stimulated and motivated to learn English via the use of technology (Butler-Pascoe & Wiburg, 2003; Freire, 2000; Traore & Kyei-Blankson, 2011). It is now commonly known that students like technology, feel comfortable with it, and enjoy using it in everyday life. All five participants realized the importance of incorporating the Internet and technology into their teaching. Thus, students had opportunities to learn through means that were appealing and exciting to them, which made the educational process more pleasant and interesting.

The five participants also realized that the use of technology had a positive impact on their teacher-student relations and allowed them to connect better to their students, which created a more teacher-student and student-student friendly atmosphere in the classroom. Students became motivated to search for materials in English online, even to watch videos and movies on their own. All the participants were pleased that after school, their students continued to be motivated to learn English.

Technology brought a multidimensional aspect to teaching and learning the English language. No matter what students watched and who they communicated with online, as long as it was in English, the students broadened their knowledge of English, contributing to what they learned during English classes.

Commonality Four: Student-Centered Teaching

During their own education in English, the five participants did not think they mattered to the teachers as all students were treated the same: strictly as passive learners whose opinions were not involved in their process of learning English. As teachers, the five participants came to the realization that students were not the same "one size fits all" student body. In fact, treating students in such a way did disservice and harm to them, as they were experiencing losing their identities and did not receive the attention they needed as students from their teachers and classmates. All the students had different needs and they needed to be treated as unique humans.

The five participants transformed themselves to "Possible Humans," more complex and integrated educators (Caine & Caine, 1997a, p. 97). Through their own passive education and experience of learning English, they gained more empathy towards their students. They realized that the students' opinions mattered, and content knowledge enriched and connected with students' experiences, interests, and opinions, contributed to gaining more knowledge in English in a more pleasant and productive way. As Coatney (2006) mentions, students need to make connections between the language and content they are learning in class and their own realities, and they will be successful in achieving goals set by teachers as they feel connected to what they are learning. The five participants also realized that it was crucial they treated classrooms as "Safe Zones" so they could risk engaging their students in discussions about difficult, touchy, and uncomfortable topics, such as death, depression, anorexia, bulimia, cyberbullying, drugs, and such.

Commonality Five: Preference for Authentic Instruction

Research demonstrates it is very challenging for EFL teachers to create an authentic English language environment for their students (Selinger, 1988; Brown, 2014). The reason for the challenge is the fact that neither the teachers, nor their students live in an environment where English is spoken as the first language.

However, I learned through the classroom observations and the interviews and that all five participants truly cared about their students and put a tremendous effort in creating an environment resembling a natural English language setting. They achieved this through using authentic teaching materials, such as authentic texts, movies, and videos. Even though the main purpose of authentic materials is to serve native English speakers (Jordan, 1997), they are also a significant vehicle for supporting the teaching and learning of English as a Foreign Language. The five participants also put effort into the esthetic part of teaching, decorating their classrooms with numerous authentic posters, maps, drawings, pictures, and images to make the process of learning for their students more genuine.

The five participants taught their students various songs and games from the English-speaking world for the same purpose, to make the process of learning more authentic and show that learning can be fun. The five participants even organized trips, language camps, and workshops to the United Kingdom and other European countries where students had opportunities to practice their knowledge of English and communicate in a natural English language environment. In this way, students could deepen and enrich their knowledge of English authentically when they used it for communication. They realized and observed that the learning of English in the classroom had a purpose, and could be genuinely utilized outside of classroom.

Limitations of the Study

All educational research is limited by the reality of how schools have to function. I, as a researcher who does not live in the country of the five participants, had limited time available for me to do my research. I was able to spend only a few hours interviewing each of the five participants, and only a few hours per week for 12 weeks observing them while they were teaching. Being constrained by time and the participants' schedules, I observed them only when time and schedules permitted, as all the five participants' schedules overlapped. As a result, the observations were neither done for all classrooms, nor for all students representing all levels of English, different grades, and ages.

In my opinion, the study would provide a more consistent picture of the observations if all five participants were observed teaching students representing the same level of English for the same amount of hours. For example, it would have been ideal if I had the possibility to observe each participant teaching students at the beginner's, intermediate, and advanced levels for five hours a week for a few months, and then perform a comparative analysis.

Suggestions for the Future Research

I recommend the five following suggestions for future research:
1. This research involves only five participants. I recommend more participants, maybe around 10. More participants may provide more opportunities to learn additional themes for comparative analysis. The increased number of participants might also contribute to finding more patterns and more objectivity in the research.

2. This research only lasted for several weeks. If a longitudinal research of several participants was done, for instance for a cycle of a full year, then richer data could be obtained. A longitudinal study might be interesting for a researcher or team of researchers who live in Poland and have continuous access to EFL schools.

3. This research involved female participants only. It would be interesting to involve males as well and observe if there are any differences between women and men and the way they approach teaching English as a Foreign Language.

4. This study involved only public high school teachers of English, and it demonstrated that the five participants represented a student-centered, authentic, technology involving approach to teaching and promoting students' speaking, communicative, and cooperative skills. It would be interesting to involve K-12 and higher education teachers of English, and investigate the approaches and methodology they represent in teaching English to their students.

5. This study involved teachers only. I would suggest doing double-sided research for the future, where not only teachers but their students were involved as well in terms of observations and interviews. In this way, the study would have a fuller and more holistic picture of what goes on behind the doors of English language classrooms, and what the correlation is between teaching and learning.

Journey as a Researcher

It is touching that the five participants so willingly agreed to participate in this 12 week-long study without any doubt and were so cooperative in making this research happen. They voluntarily let a stranger enter their lives and their classrooms, and shared information, which sometimes was very private, personal, and even painful. They let a bond and a thread of trust be built between them and myself, enriched with casual meals together, emails, and phone calls. These encounters allowed me to get to know the five participants, Anna, Barbara, Helena, Lidia, and Maria, even better.

The fact that we all were women close in age made the atmosphere of the study pleasant, creating a safe zone where I thought we all felt comfortable. Through the time spent with the five participants, I saw that they were dedicated EFL teachers with a great potential for even more creativity in the future. They proudly represented EFL public high school teachers in Poland.

Summary

In Chapter 1, I outlined the historical overview of the teaching and learning foreign language situation in Poland with a particular focus on the English language. I also defined some terms present through the course of this study. Next, I described the background of the study, including my own experience as an EFL learner and a teacher, and the political, cultural, socio-economic and educational changes that influence teaching EFL in Poland. In this chapter, I also introduced the purpose, significance, and research question of this study.

In Chapter 2, I presented three main teaching a foreign/second language approaches and demonstrated how they are connected with the research conducted in a public high school in Poland involving interviews and classroom observations of five participating Polish EFL teachers. The chapter also concentrates on other aspects of the teaching-learning dynamic, such as: a process of democratization in Poland, the use of technology in the classroom, student-centered instruction, and authentic teaching-learning. In my research I looked for the presence of the themes and how they were connected with the five research participants in their own journeys of learning the English language and how they were used in their classrooms as EFL teachers, with a particular focus on the ways the participants developed their students' speaking, communicative, and cooperative skills in English.

In Chapter 3, I demonstrated the methodology I used in doing this research. I explained the research paradigm and research approach. I described the main five participants (teachers) and secondary participants (students). Precautions to ensure the participants' privacy, anonymity, and rights were described briefly in this chapter and the participant consent forms was attached to this research in the Appendix section. This chapter also talked about research setting, the instrumentations, how and when the data was collected, analyzed, what the purpose, significance, and need of the study were to answer my research question. I explained the research design and research procedure. I pointed towards issues associated with validity of the study, the dissertation committee's involvement, and what the role the five participants played in writing this study. This chapter also connected my methodology with qualitative research literature represented by scholars such as: Yvonne S. Lincoln, Egon G. Guba, John W. Creswell, Joseph A. Maxwell, Irving Seidman, and others.

In Chapter 4, I described the five participating teachers through their interviews and class observations. I also rendered the findings of the five commonalities I found between the participants when comparing their stories from interviews and class observations. The commonalities were: participants' experience with Grammatical/Grammar-Based Approach; shift towards speaking, communicative, and cooperative skills; presence of technology in teaching; student-centered teaching; and the five participants' preference for authentic instruction.

In Chapter 5, I overviewed this study's research methodology: how I conducted the study, who my participants were, and how I designed the research. I discussed what all the commonalities meant and talked about other aspects of the study, such as revision of the methodology I used. I also reminded my readers about the context of the study, summarized the findings from Chapter 4, discussed the study's limitations, provided suggestions for future research, and reflected on my journey as a researcher.

Conclusion

Poland went through significant political, social, economic, cultural, and educational changes in the last 25 years. These changes had a profound impact on the teaching of EFL in Poland, as reflected by the experiences of the five participants: Anna, Barbara, Helena, Lidia, and Maria. I was very positively surprised and pleased with the transformation of the five participants, who left behind the Grammatical/Grammar-Based Approach of the earlier communist era. As mentioned previously, I moved to the United States 17 years ago. I was not certain what to expect in terms of English language education in Polish public schools when I started research for this study. It was an "aha moment" for me to realize how much English education has evolved and changed into a more communicative, cooperative, student-centered, authentic, and technology-involved way of teaching.

I observed and learned that the five participants came through their processes of transformation and individually came to the conclusion that they wanted to educate students, not to teach them. The difference between teaching and educating is that teaching refers to content knowledge only, and educating refers to connecting content knowledge with the reality surrounding students and teachers. The five participants chose to educate their students by connecting content knowledge with their students' realities outside of the four walls of the classroom, with the broader community, and students' interests, previous experiences, their funds of knowledge, hobbies, and opinions.

For these Polish EFL high school teachers, specifically the shift to use English as a way to pass through the gateway to Europe changed the role of English in schools. This gateway, via English, to personal, intellectual, and economic opportunities was at the center of the teacher-to-educator transformation process. Therefore, the five participants constructed assignments for their students in a way in which students could demonstrate not only what they learned from a course through textbooks, presentations, and other materials, but also what the students' reflections on the content materials were, what they meant to the students, and how the students applied the materials to their real life situations.

I believe this study, despite its imperfections and limitations, will be a valuable and a meaningful source of information for teachers and educators who will be able to see the benefits of an approach to teaching English as a Foreign Language that is communicative (with a specific focus on the development of students' speaking skills), cooperative, student-centered, and authentic, including the use of technology in teaching and learning English.

References

Apple, M. (2004). *Ideology and curriculum*. New York, NY: RoutledgeFalmer.

Ball, A. (2001–2005). *Six feet under*. Retrieved from http://www.imdb.com/title/tt0248654/?ref_=nv_sr_1

Bancroft, W. J. (1972, February). The psychology of suggestopedia or learning without stress. *The Educational Courier, 42*(4), 16–19.

Barba, R. (1997). *Science in the multicultural classroom: A guide to teaching and learning* (2nd ed.). London: Pearson.

Barooah, J. (2013). Most Catholic countries worldwide, increase seen in global south. *The Huffington Post*. Retrieved from http://www.huffingtonpost.com/2013/02/25/most-catholic-countries-top-10-by-population_n_2740237.html

Becker, H. S. (1970). *Sociological work: Method and substance*. New Brunswick, NJ: Transaction Books.

Becker, H. S., & Geer, B. (1957). Participant observation and interviewing: A comparison. *Human Organization, 16*, 28–32.

Bell, J. (2004). *Teaching multilevel classes in ESL*. Toronto: Pippin.

Berns, M. (1995). English in the European Union. *English Today, 43*(11), 3–11.

Blair, N. (2012). *Technology integration for the new 21st century learner: Today's students need educators to re-envision the role of technology in the classroom*. Retrieved from http://www.naesp.org/principal-januaryfebruary-2012-technology/technology-integration-new-21st-century-learner

Blair, R. (Ed.). (1982). *Innovative approaches to language teaching*. Rowley, MA: Newbury House.

Bogaj, A., Kwiatkowski, S. M., & Szymanski, M. J. (1999). *Education in Poland in the process of social changes*. Warsaw: Institute for Educational Research.

Boonkit, K. (2010). Enhancing the development of speaking skills for non-native speakers of English. *Procedia Social and Behavioral Sciences, 2*, 1305–1309.

Bowman, J., & Plaisir, J. (1996). Technology approaches to teaching ESL students. *Media & Methods, 32*(3), 26–27.

British Council. (1986). *English teaching profile: Poland. London: English language and literature division*. Candidate Countries Eurobarometer 2001 (2002). Brussels: European Commission. Retrieved from http://europa.eu.int/comm/public/_opinion/archives/cceb/2001/cceb20011-en.pdf

Brooks, J. G., & Brooks, M. G. (2000). *In search of understanding: The case for constructivist classrooms*. Upper Saddle River, NJ: Prentice Hall.

Brown, D. H. (2006). *Principles of learning and teaching* (5th ed.). White Plains, NY: Pearson Education ESL.

Brown, D. H. (2014). *Principle of learning and teaching: A course in second language acquisition* (6th ed.). White Plains, NY: Pearson Education ESL.

Brown, J. K. (2008, May). Student-centered instruction: Involving students in their own education. *Music Educators Journal, 94*(5), 30–35.

Brumfit, C. (1984). *Communicative methodology in language teaching: The roles of fluency and accuracy.* Cambridge: Cambridge University Press.

Bryman, A. (1988). *Quantity and quality in social research.* London: Unwin Hyman.

Butler-Pascoe, M. E., & Wiburg, K. M. (2003). *Technology and teaching English language learners.* Boston, MA: Pearson.

Buzan, T. (1983). *Use both sides of your brain: New techniques to help you read efficiently, study effectively, solve problems, remember more, think clearly.* New York, NY: E. P. Dutton.

Caine, R. N., & Caine, G. (1997a). *Education on the edge of possibility.* Alexandria, VA: ASCD.

Caine, R. N., & Caine, G. (1997b). *Unleashing the power of perceptual change: The potential of brain-based teaching.* Alexandria, VA: ASCD.

Cambridge English Proficiency. (2015). *Brief exam guide for exams from 2015.* Retrieved from http://www.cambridgeenglish.org/images/21952-cpe-proficiency-leaflet.pdf

Canale, M. (1983). From communicative competence to communicative language pedagogy. In J. Richards & R. Schmidt (Eds.), *Language and communication* (pp. 2–27). New York, NY: Longman.

Celce-Murcía, M. (2001). *Teaching English as a second or foreign language* (3rd ed.). Boston, MA: Heinle & Heinle.

Cenoz, J., & Jessner, U. (2000). *English in Europe: The acquisition of a third language.* Clevedon: Multilingual Matters.

Chavez, M. (1998). Learner's perspectives on authenticity. *International Review of Applied Linguistics in Language Teaching, 36*(4), 277–306.

Coatney, S. (2006). The importance of background knowledge. *Teacher Librarian, 34*(1), 60.

Colorado Department of Education. (2011, January). *Implementing CALLA: Cognitive Academic Language Learning Approach.* Retrieved from http://www.cde.state.co.us/sites/default/files/documents/cdesped/download/pdf/ff-calla.pdf

Coyne, I. T. (1997). Sampling in qualitative research. Purposeful and theoretical sampling; Merging or clear boundaries? *Journal of Advanced Nursing, 26*, 623–630.

Creswell, J. W. (2007). *Qualitative inquiry and research design: Choosing among five designs* (2nd ed.). Thousand Oaks, CA: Sage Publications.

Crowell, S., Caine, R. N., & Caine, G. (1998). *The re-enchantment of learning: A manual for teacher renewal and classroom transformation.* Tucson, AZ: Zephyr Press.

Crystal, D. (2003). *A dictionary of linguistics and phonetics.* Malden, MA: Blackwell.

Crystal, D. (2012). *English as a global language* (2nd ed.). New York, NY: Cambridge University Press.

Cummins, J. (1991). Language development and academic learning. In L. Malave & G. Duquette (Eds.), *Language, culture and cognition.* Clevedon: Multilingual Matters.

Cummins, J. (2001). Instructional conditions for trilingual development. *International Journal of Bilingual Education and Bilingualism, 4*(1), 61–75.

Czura, A., & Papaja, K. (2013). Curricular models of CLIL education in Poland. *International Journal of Bilingual Education and Bilingualism, 16*(3), 321–333.

Dąbrowski, M., & Wiśniewski, J. (2011). Translating key competences into the school curriculum: Lessons from the Polish experience. *European Journal of Education, 46*(3), 323–334.

DelliCarpini, M. (2008). Teacher collaboration for ESL/EFL academic success. *The Internet TESL Journal, 14*(8). Retrieved from http://iteslj.org/Techniques/DelliCarpini-TeacherCollaboration.html

Denzin, N. K., & Lincoln, Y. S. (2005). *The Sage handbook of qualitative research* (3rd ed.). Thousand Oaks, CA: Sage Publications.

Dewey, J. (1997). *Democracy and education.* New York, NY: Free Press. (Original work published in 1916)

Dewey, J. (2011). *My pedagogic creed.* Michigan, IL: University of Michigan Libraries. (Original work published in 1897)

Dexter, M. L. (2006). *Elite and specialized interviewing.* Colchester: ECP Press.

Dictionary.com. (n.d.). *Realia.* Retrieved from http://dictionary.reference.com/browse/realia

Dushku, S. (1998). English in Albania: Contact and convergence. *World Englishes, 17*(3), 369–379.

Education across Europe. (2003). *Luxembourg: Office for official publications of the European communities.* Retrieved from http://europe.eu.int/comm/eurostat/Public/datashop/print-product/EN?catalogue=Eurostat&product=KS-58-04-869-__-N-EN&mode=download

Ehrenhalt, E. (1990, March 27–30). *New tasks for teachers of English in Poland in light of social, economic, and political changes.* Paper presented at the 24th Annual Meeting of the International Association of Teachers of English as a Foreign Language, Dublin, Ireland. Retrieved from ERIC database (326067).

Eisenhardt, K. M. (1989). Building theories from case study research. *Academy of Management Review, 12*(4), 532–550.

Ellis, R. (2009). Task-based language teaching: Sorting out the misunderstandings. *International Journal of Applied Linguistics, 19*(3), 221–246.

Elman, J., Bates, E. A., & Johnson, M., Karmiloff-Smith, A., Parisi, D., & Plunkett, K. (1997). *Rethinking innateness: A connectionist perspective on development* (Neural Network Modeling and Connectionism). Cambridge, MA: MIT Press.

Erlandson, D. A., Harris, E. L., Skipper, B. L., & Allen, S. D. (1993). *Doing naturalistic inquiry: A guide to methods.* Newbury Park, CA: Sage Publications.

European Council. (2002). Barcelona European Council. *Presidency conclusions.* Press Release 100/1/02.

Evans, V. (2015). *Use of English*. Kraków: Egis.

Evans, V., & Dooley, J. (2007). *Upstream intermediate*. Newbury: Express.

Evans, V., & Edwards, L. (2008). *Upstream advanced*. Newbury: Express.

Finocchiaro, M., & Brumfit, C. (1983). *The functional-notional approach: From theory to practice*. New York, NY: Oxford University Press.

Fisiak, J. (1985). *Poznań: Uniwersytet Im. Adama Mickiewicza w Poznaniu*. Poland: Adam Mickiewicz University in Poznań.

Fisiak, J. (1994). Training English language teachers in Poland: Recent reform and its future prospects. In C. Gough & A. Jankowska (Eds.), *Directions toward 2000: Guidelines for the teaching of English in Poland* (pp. 7–15). Poznań: Instytut Filologii Angielskiej (English Philology Institute).

Fonzari, L. (1999). English in the Estonian multicultural society. *World Englishes, 18*(1), 39–48.

Freeman, D., & Freeman, Y. (1988). *Sheltered English instruction* (ERIC Digest). Retrieved from https://www.eric.ed.gov

Freire, P. (2000). *Pedagogy of freedom: Ethics, democracy and civic courage*. Boulder, CO: Rowman & Littlefield.

Gagné, E. D., Yekovich, C. W., & Yekovich, F. R. (1993). *The cognitive psychology of school learning* (2nd ed.). New York, NY: Harper Collins College Publishers.

Gattegno, C. (1970). *What we owe children: The subordination of teaching to learning*. Toronto: Educational Solutions.

Gattegno, C. (1982). Much language and little vocabulary. In R. Blair (Ed.), *Innovative approaches to language teaching* (pp. 273–292). Rowley, MA: Newbury House.

Gersick, C. (1988). Time and transition in work teams: Toward a new model of group development. *Academy of Management Journal, 31*, 9–41.

Glassheim, E. (2006, March). Ethnic cleansing, communism, and environmental devastation, 1945–1989. *The Journal of Modern History, 78*(1), 65–92.

Guariento, W., & Morley, J. (2001). Text and task authenticity in the EFL classroom. *ELT Journal, 55*(4), 347–353.

Harris, S., & Sutton, R. (1986). Functions of parting ceremonies in dying organizations. *Academy of Management Journal, 29*, 5–30.

Hayman, H. H., Cobb, W. J., Fledman, J. J., Hart, C. W., & Stember, C. H. (1954). *Interviewing in social research*. Chicago, IL: University of Chicago Press.

Heath Brice, S., & Street, B. (2008). *Ethnography: Approaches to language and literacy research*. New York, NY: Teachers College Press.

Hellermann, J. (2007). The development of practices for action in classroom dyadic interaction: Focus on task openings. *Modern Language Journal, 91*(1), 557–570.

Herrera, S. G., Kavimandan, S. K., & Holmes, M. A. (2011). *Crossing the vocabulary bridge: Differentiated strategies for diverse secondary classrooms*. New York, NY: Teachers College Press.

Herrera, S. G., & Murry, K. G. (2011). *Mastering ESL and bilingual methods: Differenti-ated instruction for Culturally and Linguistically Diverse (CLD) students*. Boston, MA: Pearson.

Hymes, D. H. (1972). On communicative competence. In J. B. Pride & J. Holmes (Eds.), *Sociolinguistics* (pp. 269–293). Baltimore, MD: Penguin Books Ltd.

Janowski, A. (1992). Polish education: Changes and prospects. *Oxford Studies in Comparative Education, 2*(1), 41–55.

Jordan, R. R. (1997). *English for academic purposes: A guide and resource for teachers*. Cambridge: Cambridge University Press.

Joubish, M. F., Khurram, M. A., Fatima, A. A., & Haider, K. (2011). Paradigms and characteristics of a good qualitative research. *World Applied Sciences Journal, 12*(11), 2082–2087.

Kallenberger, C. (2011). Retrieved from http://www.myseveralworlds.com/2011/05/16/the-esl-educators-guide-the-difference-between-eslefl-teaching-methodologies/

Kawulich, B. (2005). Participant observation as a data collection method. *Forum: Qualitative Social Research, 6*(2), 43. Retrieved from http://www.qualitative-research.net/index.php/fqs/article/view/466/996#g2

Kelly, L. G. (1976). *25 centuries of language teaching*. Rowley, MA: Newbury House.

Kidder, T. (1982). *Soul of a new machine*. New York, NY: Avon.

Kielar, B. (1972). Behind the curtain: English in Poland. In J. McCulloch (Ed.), *English around the world number 6*. Eric Document 066 085.

Kilickaya, F. (2004). Authentic materials and cultural content in EFL classrooms. *The Internet TESL Journal, 10*(7), 1–6. Retrieved from http://iteslj.org/Techniques/Kilickaya-Autentic Material.html

Klancar, N. I. (2006). Developing speaking skills in the young learners' classroom. *The Internet TESL Journal, 12*(11). Retrieved from http://iteslj.org/Techniques/Klancar-SpeakingSkills.html

Krashen, S. D. (1981). *Second language acquisition and second language learning*. London: Pergamon Press.

Krukiewicz-Gacek, A., Griffith, K. G., Skrynicka-Knapczyk, D., Butler, N. L., & Kristonis, W. A. (2007). Should we teach English for work purposes to undergraduates at Polish higher schools? *The Lamar University Electronic Journal of Student Research*. Retrieved from http://files.eric.ed.gov/fulltext/ED495376.pdf

Kuhn, T. S. (1996). *The structure of scientific revolutions* (3rd ed.). Chicago, IL: The University of Chicago Press.

Larsen-Freeman, D. (2000). *Techniques and principles in language teaching*. New York, NY: OUP.

Larsen-Freeman, D. (2011). *Techniques and principles in language learning. Teaching techniques in English as a second language* (3rd ed.). Oxford: Oxford University Press.

Lekki, P. (2003). Watch your language. *The Warsaw Voice*. Retrieved from http://www.warsawvoice.pl/view/2875

Li, D. (1998). "It's always more difficult than you plan and imagine": Teachers' perceived difficulties in introducing the communicative approach in South Korea. *TESOL Quarterly, 32*(4), 677–703.

Lincoln, Y. S., & Guba, E. G. (1985). *Naturalistic inquiry* (1st ed.). Beverly Hills, CA: Sage Publications.

Lingua franca – Definition of lingua franca in English from the Oxford dictionary. Retrieved from http://www.oxforddictionaries.com/definition/english/lingua-franca

Lozanov, G. (1982). Suggestology and suggestopedia: Theory and practice. In R. Blair (Ed.), *Innovative approaches to language teaching* (pp. 146–159). Rowley, MA: Newbury House.

Marshall, C., & Rossman, G. B. (1989). *Designing qualitative research*. Newbury Park, CA: Sage Publications.

Maxwell, J. A. (2008). Designing a qualitative study. In L. Bickman (Ed.), *Applied research designs* (pp. 214–253). Thousand Oaks, CA: Sage Publications.

Mayer, W. V. (1996). Biology education in the United States during the twentieth century. *The Quarterly Review of Biology, 61*(4), 481–507.

McCallen, B. (1991). *English in Eastern Europe* (Special Report No. 2075). London: The Economist Intelligence Unit.

McCombs, B. L., & Whisler, J. S. (1997). *The learner-centered classroom and school: Strategies for increasing student motivation and achievement*. San Francisco, CA: Jossey-Bass.

McKinley, S., Hastings, B., & Raczyńska, R. (2012). *New matura success*. Warszawa, Poland: Longman/Pearson.

Merriam, S. (1991). *Case study research in education: A qualitative approach*. San Francisco, CA: Jossey-Bass.

Mishler, E. G. (1979). Research interviewing. *Harvard Educational Review, 49*(1), 1–19.

Morris, F. A., & Tarone, E. E. (2003). Impact of classroom dynamics on the effectiveness of recasts in second language acquisition. *Language Learning, 53*, 325–368.

Muchisky, D. (1985). *The unnatural approach: Language learning in Poland*. Retrieved from ERIC Database (ED 264728).

Newell, M. (1994). *Four weddings and a funeral*. Retrieved from http://www.imdb.com/title/tt0109831/?ref_=fn_al_tt_1

Nunan, D. (1992). *Research methods in language learning*. New York, NY: CUP.

Odrowaz, E. (2009). *Collapse of communism started in Poland*. Retrieved from http://www.theepochtimes.com/n2/opinion/collapse-of-communism-started-in-poland-24965.html

O'Farrell, M. (2005). Abuse of Polish workers widespread, says embassy. *Irish Examiner*. Retrieved from http://www.irishexaminer.com/archives/2005/0224/ireland/abuse-of-polish-workers-widespread-says-embassy-130329102.html

O'Malley, J. M., & Chamot, A. U. (1990). *Learning strategies in a second language acquisition*. New York, NY: Cambridge University Press.

O'Reilly, L. (1998). English language cultures in Bulgaria: A linguistic sibling rivalry? *World Englishes, 17*(1), 71–84.

Ovando, C., & Collier, V. (2011). *Bilingual and ESL classroom: Teaching in multicultural contexts* (5th ed.). Boston, MA: McGraw-Hill.

Petzold, R., & Berns, M. (2000). Catching up with Europe: Speakers and functions of English in Hungary. *World Englishes, 19*(1), 113–124.

Peyton, J. K., Moore, S. C. K., & Young, S. (2010, April). Evidence-based, student-centered instructional practices. *Center for Applied Linguistics*, 1–8.

Phillipson, R., & Skutnabb-Kangas, T. (1997). Linguistic human rights and English in Europe. *World Englishes, 16*(1), 27–43.

Pinfield, L. (1986). A field evaluation of perspectives on organizational decision making. *Administrative Science Quarterly, 31*, 365–388.

Pulver, A. (2015). Oscar for best foreign film. *The Guardian*. Retrieved from http://www.theguardian.com/film/2015/feb/23/ida-wins-oscar-for-best-foreign-language-film

Reichelt, M. (2005). English in Poland. *World Englishes, 24*(2), 217–225.

Richard, J. C. (2001). *Curriculum development in language teaching*. Cambridge: Cambridge University Press.

Richards, J. C., & Rogers, T. (1986). *Approaches and methods in language teaching*. New York, NY: Cambridge University Press.

Richards, J. C., & Rogers, T. (2014). *Approaches and methods in language teaching* (3rd ed.). New York, NY: Cambridge University Press.

Riche, G. (2009). *Sherlock Holmes*. Retrieved from http://www.imdb.com/title/tt0988045/?ref_=fn_al_tt_1

Savignon, S. J. (1983). *Communicative competence: Theory and classroom practice*. Reading, MA: Addison Wesley.

Schatzman, L., & Strauss, A. L. (1973). *Field research: Strategies for a natural sociology*. Englewood Cliffs, NJ: New Prentice Hall.

Schensul, S. L., Schensul, J. J., & LeCompte, M. D. (1999). *Essential ethnographic methods: Observations, interviews, and questionnaires* (Book 2 in Ethnographer's Toolkit). Walnut Creek, CA: AltaMira Press.

Schlechty, P. C. (2011). No community left behind. In A. C. Ornstein, E. F. Pajak, & S. B. Ornstein (Eds.), *Contemporary issues in curriculum* (pp. 41–52). Upper Saddle River, NJ: Pearson.

Schleppegrell, M. (1991, March). *Teaching English in Central Europe*. Paper presented at the 25th Annual Meeting of the Teachers of English to Speakers of Other Languages, New York, NY. Retrieved from ERIC Database (ED 333724).

Schultz, F. (2013). Whose quote is that, really? *Gazettextra*. Retrieved from http://www.gazettextra.com/weblogs/word-badger/2013/mar/24/whose-quote-really/

Seidman, I. (2013). *Interviewing as qualitative research: A guide for researchers in education and the social sciences* (4th ed.). New York, NY: Teachers College.

Shanahan, D. (1997). Articulating the relationship between language, literature and culture: Toward a new agenda for foreign language teaching and research. *The Modern Language Journal, 81*(2), 164–174.

Shuell, T. J. (1986). Cognitive conceptions of learning. *Review of Educational Research, 56*, 411–436.

Seliger, H. (1988). Psycholinguistic issues in second language acquisition. In L. M. Beebe (Ed.), *Issues in second language acquisition* (pp. 17–40). New York, NY: Newbury House Publishers.

Spiteri, D. (2010). Back to the classroom: Lessons learnt by a teacher educator. *Studying Teacher Education, 6*(2), 131–141.

Stuart, G., & Nocon, H. (1996). Second culture acquisition: Ethnography in the foreign language classroom. *The Modern Language Journal, 80*(4), 431–449.

TEFL survival. (n.d.). *Teach English! Make a splash in the world! Realia.* Retrieved from http://www.teflsurvival.com/teaching-aids.html

Terrell, T. (1991). The natural approach in bilingual education. In C. Leyba (Ed.), *Schooling and language minority students: A theoretical framework.* Los Angeles, CA: Evaluation, Dissemination and Assessment Center.

Terrell, T., Egasse, J., & Voge, W. (1982). Techniques for a more natural approach to second language acquisition and learning. In R. Blair (Ed.), *Innovative approaches to language teaching* (pp. 174–175). Rowley, MA: Newbury House.

Thompson, J. R. (2004). *The entry of Poland into the European Union: Moving the center to the periphery.* Retrieved from http://www.ruf.rice.edu/~sarmatia/404/242thomp.html

Tobias, S. (1992). *Revitalizing undergraduate science: Why some things work and most don't.* Tucson, AZ: Research Corporation.

TOEFL. (2005/2006). *Test and score data summary for TOEFL Internet-based test: September 2005-December 2006 test data. Test of English as a foreign language.* Retrieved from http://www.ets.org/Media/Research/pdf/TOEFL-SUM-0506-iBT.pdf

Trading Economics. (2015). *Poland unemployment rate.* Retrieved from http://www.tradingeconomics.com/poland/unemployment-rate

Traore, M., & Kyei-Blankson, L. (2011). Using literature and multiple technologies in ESL instruction. *Journal of Language Teaching and Research, 2*(3), 561–568.

Tseng, Y. (2002). A lesson in culture. *ELT Journal, 56*(1), 11–21.

Umińska, M., Hastings, B., Chandler, D., Fricker, R., & Trapnell, B. (2014). *English: Repetytorium maturalne.* Warszawa, Poland: Longman/Pearson.

University of English ESOL Examinations. (2011). *Cambridge English first.* Retrieved from http://www.cambridgeenglish.org/images/25091-fce-level-b2-document.pdf

Van Essen, A. (1997). English in mainland Europe: A Dutch perspective. *World Englishes, 16*(1), 95–103. Retrieved from http://www.ruf.rice.edu/~sarmatia/404/242thomp.html

Varney, M. H. (1984). Poland: Another kind of hunger. *The Incorporated Linguist, 23*(3), 155.

Volenski, L. T., & Grzymala-Moszczynska, H. (1997). Religious pluralism in Poland. *America, 176*(6), 21–23.

Vygotsky, L. S. (1978). *Mind in society: The development of higher psychological processes* (M. Cole, V. John-Steiner, S. Scriber, & E. Souberman, Eds.). Cambridge, MA: Harvard University Press. (Original work published in 1934)

Weinstein, G. (1999). *Learners' lives as curriculum: Six journeys to immigrant literacy.* Washington, DC & McHenry, IL: Center for Applied Linguistics and Delta Systems.

Weir, P. (1989). *Dead poets' society.* Retrieved from http://www.imdb.com/title/tt0097165/

Wierbińska, D. (2009). A profile of an effective teacher of English: A qualitative study from Poland. *Hacettepe Üniversitesi Eğitim Fakültesi Dergisi* (Hacettepe University Journal of Education), *36*, 306–315.

Wines, M. (2003). New study supports idea Stalin was poisoned. *The New York Times.* Retrieved from http://www.nytimes.com/2003/03/05/world/study-supports-idea-stalin-was-poisoned.html?pagewanted=all

Wong Fillmore, L., & Valadez, C. (1986). Teaching bilingual learners. In M. C. Wittrock (Ed.), *Handbook of research on teaching* (3rd ed., pp. 648–685). New York, NY: Longman.

Yosso, T. (2002, Spring). Critical race media literacy: Challenging deficit discourse about Chicanas/os. *Journal of Popular Film and Television, 30*(1), 52–62.

Zaremba, A. J. (2006). *Speaking professionally.* Canada: Thompson South-Western.

Zemeckis, R. (2009). *A Christmas carol.* Retrieved from http://www.imdb.com/title/tt1067106/?ref_=nv_sr_1

Zhang, Y. (2009). Reading to speak: Integrating oral communication skills. *English Teaching Forum, 47*(1), 32–34. Retrieved from http://exchanges.state.gov/englishteaching/forum/archives/2009/09-47-1.html

Zimmerman, L. (2010). *ESL, EFL, and bilingual education: Exploring historical, socio-cultural, linguistic, and instructional foundations.* Charlotte, NC: Information Age Publishing.